APPLYING KNOWLEDGE AND SKILLS

Higher BIOLOGY

for CfE

Writing Team:

James Torrance

James Fullarton

Clare Marsh

James Simms

Caroline Stevenson

Diagrams by **James Torrance**

Curriculum for Excellence

HODDER
GIBSON
AN HACHETTE UK COMPANY

The Publishers would like to thank the following for permission to reproduce copyright material:

Photo credits
p.1 (background) and Unit 1 running head image © 2010 Steve Allen/Brand X Pictures/photolibrary.com; p.1 (inset left) © april21st – Fotolia, (inset centre) © Dr Keith Wheeler/Science Photo Library, (inset right) James Torrance; p.27 (background) and Unit 2 running head image © Loren Rodgers – Fotolia; p.27 (inset left) © Natural Visions/Alamy, (inset centre) © Dennis Kunkel Microscopy, Inc/Visuals Unlimited, Inc., (inset right) © Dennis Kunkel Microscopy, Inc./Visuals Unlimited/Corbis; p.57 (background) and Unit 3 running head image © pro6x7 – Fotolia; p.57 (inset left) © Anna – Fotolia, (inset centre) © Jef Meul/Minden Pictures/FLPA RM, (inset right) © Oceans-Image/Photoshot.

Acknowledgements
The authors and publisher would like to extend grateful thanks to Jim Stafford for assistance offered at manuscript stage of this book, as well as for futher guidance and editorial advice during the production process.

Every effort has been made to trace all copyright holders, but if any have been inadvertently overlooked the Publishers will be pleased to make the necessary arrangements at the first opportunity.

Although every effort has been made to ensure that website addresses are correct at time of going to press, Hodder Gibson cannot be held responsible for the content of any website mentioned in this book. It is sometimes possible to find a relocated web page by typing in the address of the home page for a website in the URL window of your browser.

Hachette UK's policy is to use papers that are natural, renewable and recyclable products and made from wood grown in sustainable forests. The logging and manufacturing processes are expected to conform to the environmental regulations of the country of origin.

Orders: please contact Bookpoint Ltd, 130 Milton Park, Abingdon, Oxon OX14 4SB. Telephone: (44) 01235 827720. Fax: (44) 01235 400454. Lines are open 9.00–5.00, Monday to Saturday, with a 24-hour message answering service. Visit our website at www.hoddereducation.co.uk. Hodder Gibson can be contacted direct on: Tel: 0141 848 1609; Fax: 0141 889 6315; email: hoddergibson@hodder.co.uk

© James Torrance, James Fullarton, Clare Marsh, James Simms, Caroline Stevenson 2012
First published in 2012 by
Hodder Gibson, an imprint of Hodder Education,
An Hachette UK Company
2a Christie Street
Paisley PA1 1NB

Impression number 5 4 3
Year   2016 2015
ISBN: 978 1444 180787

Cover photo © Andy Rouse/naturepl.com
Illustrations by James Torrance
Typeset in Minion Pro 11pt by Fakenham Prepress Solutions, Fakenham, Norfolk NR21 8NN
Printed in India

A catalogue record for this title is available from the British Library

Contents

Unit 1 DNA and the Genome

1 Structure of DNA   3

2 Replication of DNA   5

3 Control of gene expression   6

4 Cellular differentiation   10

5 Structure of the genome   14

6 Mutations   16

7 Evolution   18

8 Genomic sequencing   23

Unit 2 Metabolism and Survival

9 Metabolic pathways and their control   29

10 Cellular respiration   35

11 Metabolic rate   39

12 Metabolism in conformers and regulators   42

13 Metabolism and adverse conditions   44

14 Environmental control of metabolism   48

15 Genetic control of metabolism   53

16 Ethical considerations in the use of microorganisms   56

Unit 3 Sustainability and Interdependence

17 Food supply, plant growth and productivity   61

18 Plant and animal breeding   67

19 Crop protection   73

20 Animal welfare   79

21 Symbiosis   83

22 Social behaviour   89

23 Mass extinction and biodiversity   90

24 Threats to biodiversity   93

Answers   **95**

The book you are holding is from a second (or subsequent) printing of this title. In this version, there is an additional question (Number 1) in Unit 2, Section 12, and the Chapter/Section names and page numbers above have also been amended from the first printing. These changes have been made to be in line with amendments that were made to the ordering of the Higher syllabus in summer 2014.

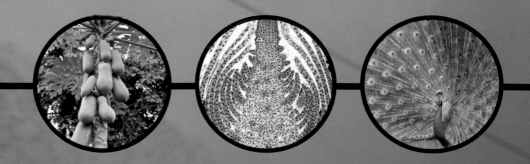

Unit 1

DNA and the Genome

1 Structure of DNA

1 Table 1.1 shows a sample of Chargaff's data following the analysis of DNA extracted from several species.

a) Study the data and calculate the figures that should have been entered in boxes X and Y. (2)

b) i) State Chargaff's rules.
ii) Do the data in the table support these rules?
iii) Explain your answer. (3)

c) With respect to the number of the different bases in a DNA sample, which of the following is correct? (1)
A C = T **B** A = G **C** A+G = C+T
D A+T = G+C

2 a) Calculate the percentage of thymine molecules present in a DNA molecule containing 1000 bases of which 200 are guanine. (1)

b) State the number of cytosine bases present in a DNA molecule which contains 10 000 base molecules of which 18% are adenine. (1)

3 Figure 1.1 shows a cell's genetic material.

a) i) Name the parts enclosed in boxes 1, 2 and 3.
ii) Which of these boxed structures contains nucleic acid and consists of many different genes?
iii) Which of these structures is one of four basic units whose order determines the information held in a gene? (5)

b) The DNA helix of one of these chromosomes is found to be 5 cm long when fully uncoiled and 5 µm long when tightly coiled.
i) Express these data as a packing ratio of fully extended DNA : tightly coiled DNA.
ii) Suggest why scientists normally express the length of a chromosome in number of base pairs. (2)

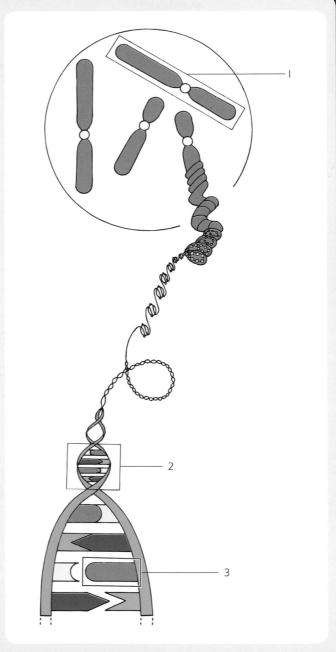

Figure 1.1

Species	%A	%C	%G	%T	A/T	G/C
chicken	28.0	21.6	**box X**	28.4	0.99	1.02
grasshopper	29.3	20.7	20.7	29.3	1.00	1.00
human	29.3	20.0	20.7	30.0	0.98	1.04
maize	26.8	23.2	22.8	27.2	0.99	**box Y**
wheat	27.3	22.8	22.7	27.2	1.00	1.00

Table 1.1

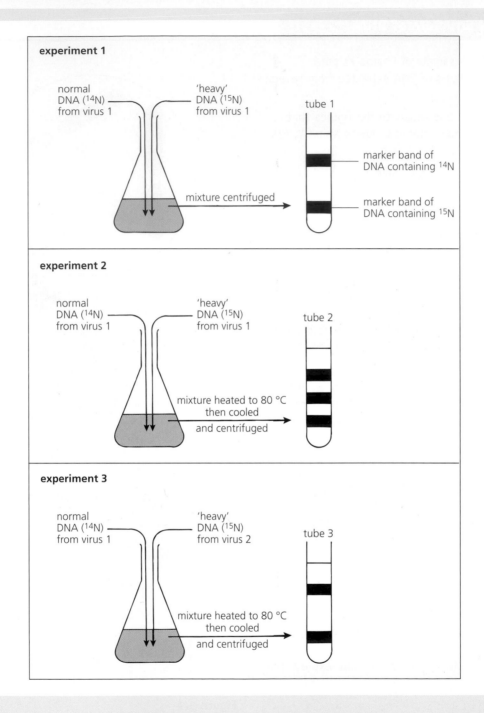

Figure 1.2

4   When DNA is heated to 80 °C, its component strands separate from one another. If the DNA is then cooled slowly, the strands become reunited as a double helix. Figure 1.2 shows a series of experiments involving the use of DNA labelled with the common isotope of nitrogen (^{14}N) and DNA labelled with the heavy isotope of nitrogen (^{15}N).

a) Explain the results obtained in tube 2. (2)

b) Explain why tube 3 has only two bands. (2)

c) By what means could scientists produce a strain of bacteriophage virus with ^{15}N in its DNA? (3)

2 Replication of DNA

1 Figure 2.1 shows a replication 'bubble' on a strand of DNA.

   a) i) Redraw the diagram including the given labels and then mark '3' end' and '5' end' on the parental DNA strand for a second time.
   ii) Draw in and label a starting point (origin of replication).
   iii) Label one of the primer molecules.
   iv) Label the leading DNA strand and a fragment of the lagging strand.
   v) Use the letter P four times to indicate all the locations where DNA polymerase would be active. (6)

   b) i) In this chromosome the replication fork moves at a rate of 2500 base pairs per minute. If this chromosome is $5×10^7$ base pairs in length, how many minutes would one replication fork take to replicate the entire chromosome?
   ii) In reality, replication of this chromosome's DNA only takes 3 minutes. Explain how this is achieved. (2)

Figure 2.1

2 The graph in Figure 2.2 shows the expected number of copies of DNA that would be generated by the polymerase chain reaction (PCR) under ideal conditions.

   a) i) What name is given to the type of graph paper used here to present the data?
   ii) Why has this type of graph paper been used? (2)

   b) How many cycles of PCR are required to produce 10 000 000 copies of the DNA? (1)

   c) How many cycles are required to increase the number of copies of DNA already present at ten cycles by a factor of 10^3? (1)

   d) i) How many copies of the DNA were present after 30 cycles?
   ii) Now state your answer in words. (2)

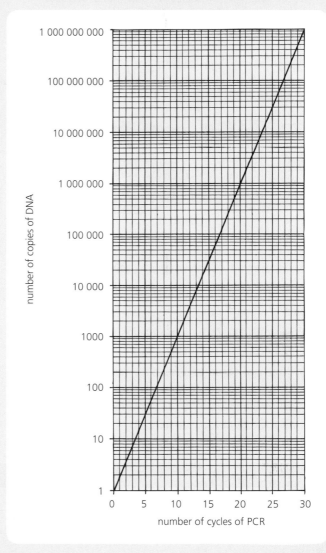

Figure 2.2

3 Describe the main processes that occur during the replication of a molecule of DNA. (9)

3 Control of gene expression

1 A particular polypeptide chain was known to be ten amino acids in length. When enzymes were used to break down several molecules of it at three different places along its length, the fragments shown in Figure 3.1 were obtained.

(Note: AA = amino acid; N = one end of the polypeptide chain.)

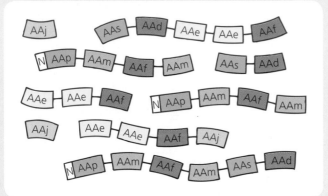

Figure 3.1

Draw a diagram of the complete polypeptide chain. (1)

2 Figure 3.2 shows a chromatogram of three amino acids (X, Y and Z).

a) Identify the three amino acids with the aid of Table 2.1. (3)

b) Which of these amino acids was
   i) most soluble in the solvent?
   ii) least soluble in the solvent?
   iii) Explain your answer. (2)

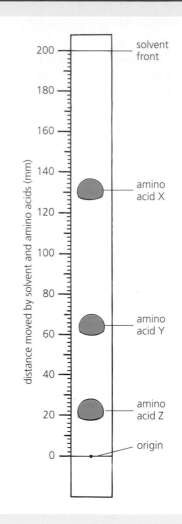

Figure 3.2

Amino acid	Abbreviation	Rf	Amino acid	Abbreviation	Rf
histidine	his	0.11	cysteine	cys	0.40
glutamine	glun	0.13	proline	pro	0.43
lysine	lys	0.14	tyrosine	tyr	0.45
arginine	arg	0.20	asparagine	aspn	0.50
aspartic acid	asp	0.24	methionine	met	0.55
glycine	gly	0.26	valine	val	0.60
serine	ser	0.27	tryptophan	tryp	0.66
glutamic acid	glu	0.30	phenylalanine	phe	0.68
threonine	thr	0.35	isoleucine	ileu	0.72
alanine	ala	0.38	leucine	leu	0.73

Table 3.1

Blood protein group		Details
albumin		It makes up more than half of the protein in blood serum and prevents blood from leaking out of vessels.
globulins	alpha-1-globulins (α1)	They include a high-density lipoprotein which contains 'good' cholesterol *not* taken into the artery wall.
	alpha-2-globulins (α2)	They include a protein that binds with haemoglobin. Some of the proteins in this group are increased in concentration in conditions such as diabetes and cirrhosis of the liver.
	beta-globulins (β)	They include a protein called transferrin that carries iron through the bloodstream and increases in concentration during iron-deficiency anaemia.
	gamma-globulins (γ)	Many are antibodies whose numbers increase in response to viral invasion and some cancers such as myeloma (which affects bone marrow) and lymphatic leukaemia.

Table 3.2

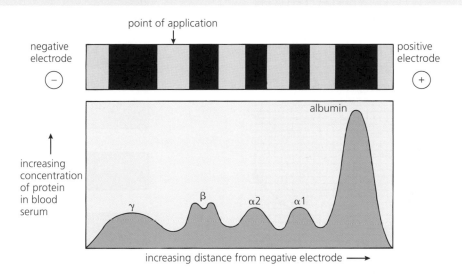

Figure 3.3

3   Human blood serum contains two major groups of protein: albumin and globulins. Some examples of these proteins are given in Table 3.2. Figure 3.3 shows a separation of serum proteins by electrophoresis and the results presented as a graph.

a) i)   Compared with the globulins as a group, do albumin proteins have a higher or a lower molecular weight?
ii)   Explain how you arrived at your answer. (2)

b) i)   Based only on the information given in Table 3.2, identify the specific group of blood proteins that could indicate liver disease if its concentration increased greatly.
ii)   From what condition might a person be suffering if the concentration of beta-globulins in their bloodstream increased to an abnormal level? (2)

c) i)   The graph in Figure 3.4 shows a patient's results from a serum protein electrophoresis test. From which of the following could this person be suffering?

(Your answer should be based only on the information in Table 3.2.)

A   leakage of blood from vessels

B   cirrhosis of the liver

C   iron-deficiency anaemia

D   cancer of cells in bone marrow.

ii)   Why is this diagnosis *not* conclusive? (2)

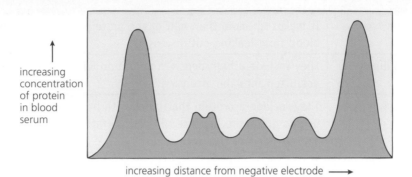

increasing concentration of protein in blood serum

increasing distance from negative electrode ⟶

Figure 3.4

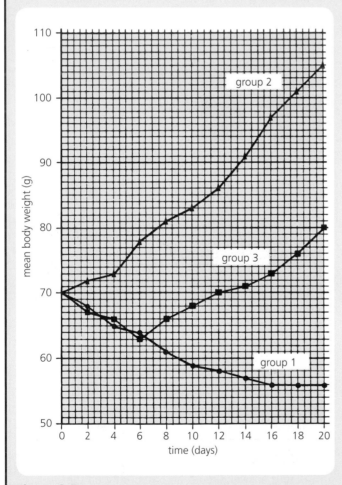

Figure 3.5

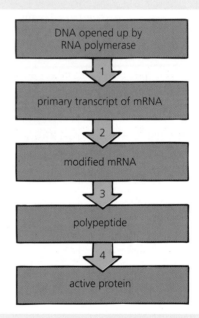

DNA opened up by RNA polymerase

1

primary transcript of mRNA

2

modified mRNA

3

polypeptide

4

active protein

Figure 3.6

experiment using rats where group 1 was fed zein (maize protein), group 2 was fed casein (milk protein) and group 3 was fed a diet which was changed at day 6.

a) One of the proteins contains all of the essential amino acids whereas the other lacks two of them.
   i) Identify each protein.
   ii) Explain how you arrived at your answer. (4)

b) i) State which protein was given to the rats in group 3 during the first 6 days of the experiment.
   ii) Suggest TWO different ways in which their diet could have been altered from day 6 onwards to account for the results shown in the graph. (3)

c) By how many grams did the mean body weight of the rats in group 2 increase over the 20-day period? (1)

4   Some amino acids can be synthesised by the body from simple compounds; others cannot be synthesised and must be supplied in the diet. The latter type are called the **essential amino acids**. The graph in Figure 3.5 shows the results of an

d) Calculate the percentage decrease in mean body weight shown by the rats in group 1 over the 20-day period. (1)

5 Figure 3.6 shows a flow chart which refers to the coding for and synthesis of an active protein. Match the numbered arrows with the following answers. (3)

a) cutting and splicing of primary transcript of mRNA

b) post-translational modification

c) transcription

d) translation.

6 The information in Table 3.3 refers to the relative numbers of ribosomes present in the cells of a new leaf developing at a shoot tip.

a) Construct an hypothesis to account for the trend shown by these data. (2)

b) Explain why the relative numbers of ribosomes in the cells of a fully grown leaf do not drop to zero. (1)

Age of new leaf (days)	Relative number of ribosomes in cells
1	300
3	500
5	650
7	450
9	210
11	200
13	200
15	200

Table 3.3

7 Figure 3.7 shows the method by which the genetic code is transmitted during protein synthesis. Table 3.4 gives some of the triplets which correspond to certain amino acids.

a) Identify bases 1–9. (2)

b) Name processes P and Q. (1)

c) Copy and complete Table 3.4. (2)

d) Give the triplet of bases that would be exposed on a molecule of tRNA to which valine would become attached. (1)

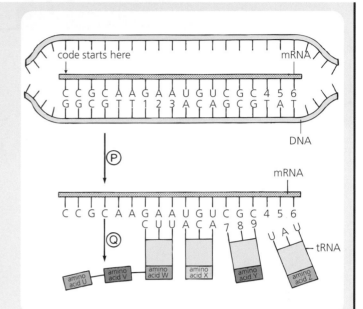

Figure 3.7

e) Use your table to identify amino acids U, V, W, X, Y and Z. (2)

f) i) Work out the mRNA code for part of a polypeptide chain with the amino acid sequence:

threonine–leucine–alanine–glycine.

ii) State the genetic code on the DNA strand from which this mRNA would be formed. (2)

Amino acid	Codon	Anticodon
alanine		CGC
arginine	CGC	
cysteine		ACA
glutamic acid	GAA	
glutamine		GUU
glycine	GGC	
isoleucine		UAU
leucine	CUU	
proline		GGC
threonine	ACA	
tyrosine		AUA
valine	GUU	

Table 3.4

8 Give an account of translation of mRNA into a polypeptide. (9)

4 Cellular differentiation

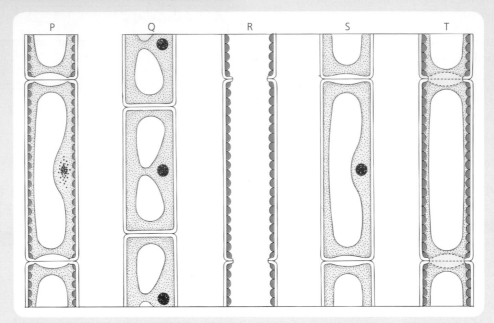

Figure 4.1

1 Figure 4.1 shows five stages in the development of a xylem vessel.

   a) Arrange them in the correct order starting with Q. (1)

   b) Which stages contain cytoplasm? (1)

   c) i) Which stage shows a fully differentiated xylem vessel?
   ii) Identify the TWO features shown in the diagram that led to your choice.
   iii) Relate each of these to a function performed by xylem. (5)

2 Figure 4.2 shows a transverse section of a young tree.

   a) Is the cambium an *apical* or a *lateral* meristem? (1)

   b) How old is this tree? (1)

   c) During which year were the conditions most suitable for the differentiation of woody xylem from cambium? (1)

   d) i) Identify the year during which the tree's leaves were heavily infested with insect larvae.
   ii) Explain how you arrived at your answer. (2)

3 Figure 4.3 shows an early tissue-culturing experiment involving the carrot plant.

   Match arrows 1–5 with the following steps in the procedure. (4)

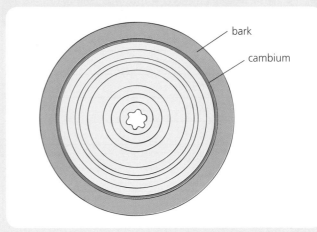

Figure 4.2

   a) 'embryoids' removed from liquid culture medium

   b) fragments containing living cells cut out of carrot root

   c) plantlets transferred to fertile soil where they grow into adult plants

   d) root fragments transferred to liquid culture medium where they become 'embryoids'

   e) 'embryoids' planted in sterile nutrient agar where they become plantlets.

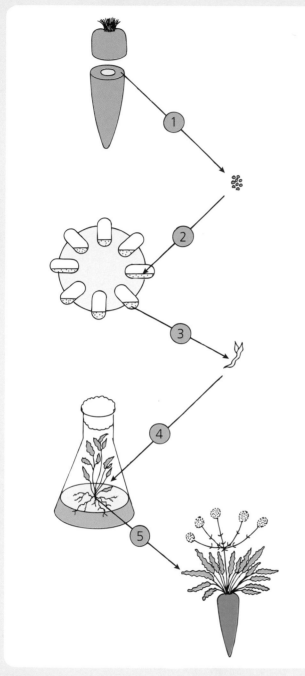

Figure 4.3

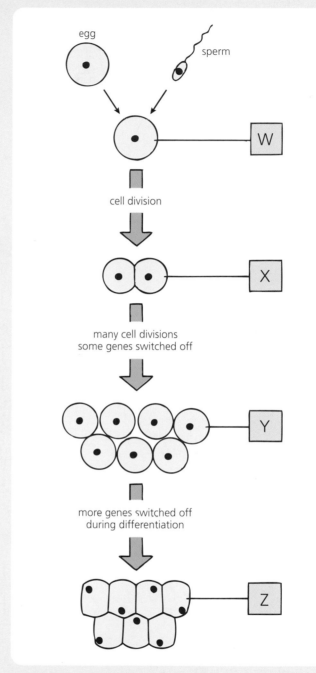

Figure 4.4

4 Figure 4.4 represents the processes of cell division and cellular differentiation in an animal.

Match W, X, Y and Z with the following terms: *specialised cell, zygote, tissue (adult) stem cell* and *embryonic stem cell*. (3)

5 The procedure that was adopted to produce 'Dolly the sheep' is shown in Figure 4.5.

a) What name is given to the technique employed to create the original cell which gave rise to Dolly? (1)

b) Why is Dolly said to be the result of a *cloning* procedure? (1)

c) i) Did Dolly develop a black face or a white face?
   ii) Explain your answer. (2)

d) i) What was the chance of Dolly being a ram?
   A 0 B 1 in 1 C 1 in 2
   ii) Explain your choice of answer. (2)

→

11

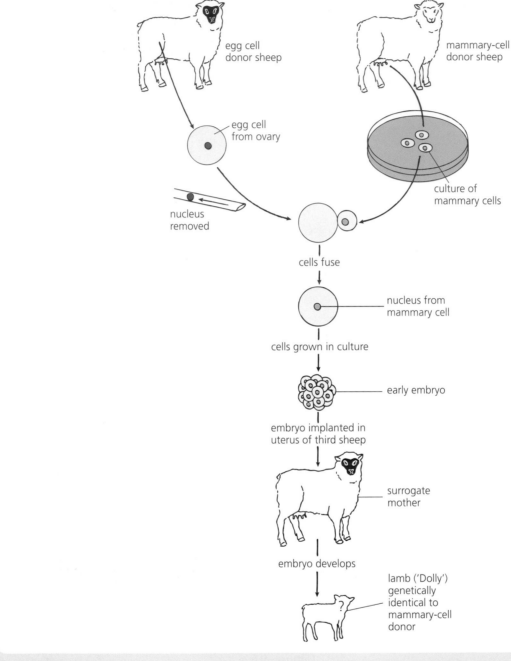

Figure 4.5

6 The ten statements shown in Figure 4.6 were made by people interviewed about the use of human embryos for stem cell research.

   a) Classify the statements into two groups:
     i) those in favour of this type of research
     ii) those opposed to this type of research. (2)

   b) What would your position have been in this ethical debate if you had been interviewed?

7 The four people shown in Figure 4.7 all support the use of human embryos in stem cell research.

   a) Who is making a statement based on fact rather than expressing an opinion? (1)

   b) i) Do you consider this person's statement to be a convincing or an unconvincing argument in support of the use of embryonic stem cells for research?
     ii) Justify your answer. (2)

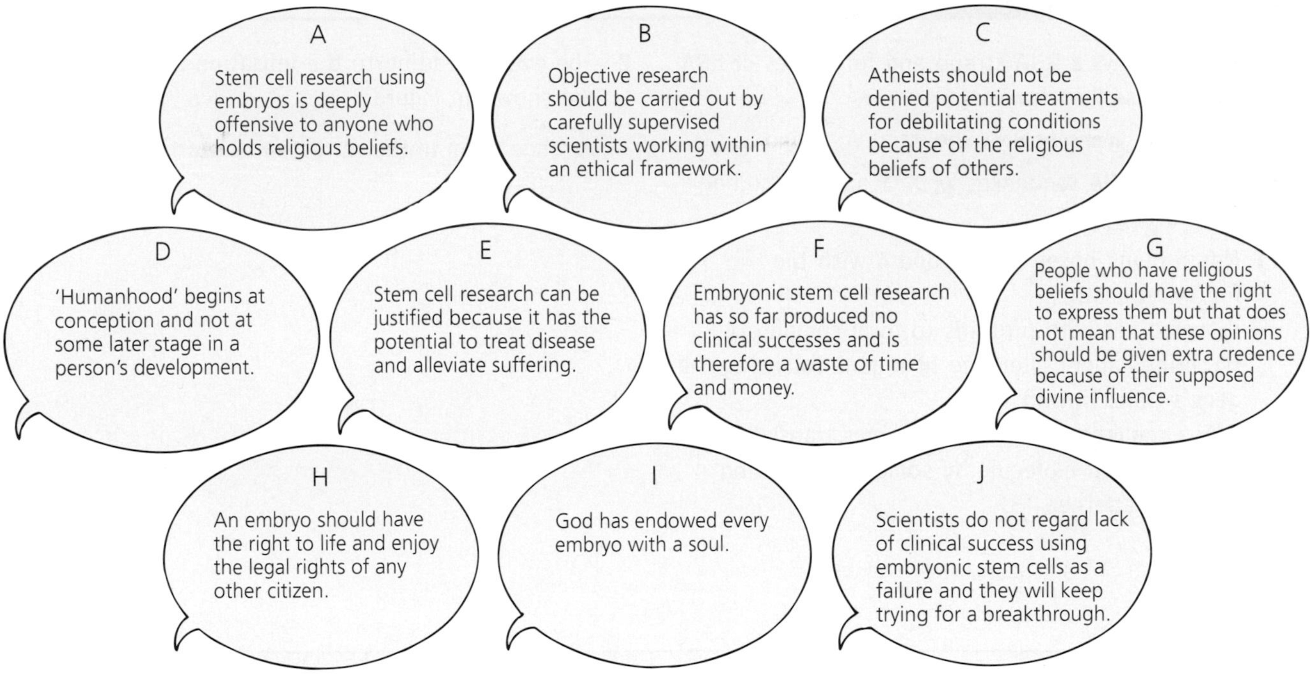

A: Stem cell research using embryos is deeply offensive to anyone who holds religious beliefs.

B: Objective research should be carried out by carefully supervised scientists working within an ethical framework.

C: Atheists should not be denied potential treatments for debilitating conditions because of the religious beliefs of others.

D: 'Humanhood' begins at conception and not at some later stage in a person's development.

E: Stem cell research can be justified because it has the potential to treat disease and alleviate suffering.

F: Embryonic stem cell research has so far produced no clinical successes and is therefore a waste of time and money.

G: People who have religious beliefs should have the right to express them but that does not mean that these opinions should be given extra credence because of their supposed divine influence.

H: An embryo should have the right to life and enjoy the legal rights of any other citizen.

I: God has endowed every embryo with a soul.

J: Scientists do not regard lack of clinical success using embryonic stem cells as a failure and they will keep trying for a breakthrough.

Figure 4.6

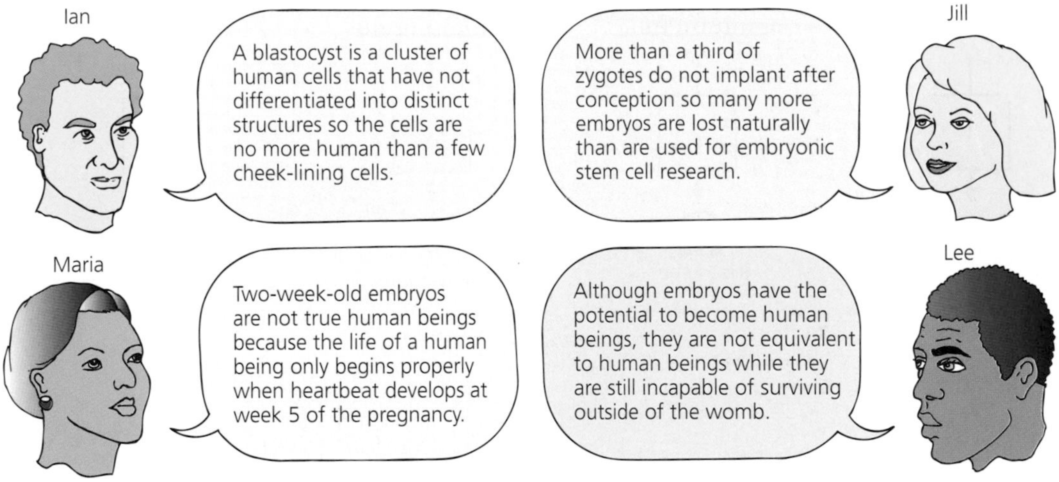

Ian: A blastocyst is a cluster of human cells that have not differentiated into distinct structures so the cells are no more human than a few cheek-lining cells.

Jill: More than a third of zygotes do not implant after conception so many more embryos are lost naturally than are used for embryonic stem cell research.

Maria: Two-week-old embryos are not true human beings because the life of a human being only begins properly when heartbeat develops at week 5 of the pregnancy.

Lee: Although embryos have the potential to become human beings, they are not equivalent to human beings while they are still incapable of surviving outside of the womb.

Figure 4.7

8 Give an account of the two types of stem cell and their research and therapeutic value. (9)

5 Structure of the genome

1 Figure 5.1 shows a DNA strand and four types of RNA that are transcribed from it.

a) Name the types of RNA shown at A, B and C. (3)

b) Which of DNA sequences W, X, Y and Z is coding for protein? (1)

c) Match blank boxes 1, 2, 3 and 4 with the following answers:
i) combines with proteins to form complexes
ii) brings about silencing of a gene following the gene's transcription
iii) a sequence of codons becomes translated
iv) folding of molecule by some bases pairing with one another. (3)

2 The events leading to the initiation of transcription are shown in Figure 5.2.

Arrange them in the correct order starting with A. (1)

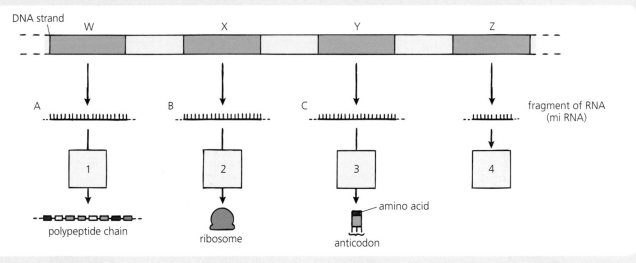

Figure 5.1

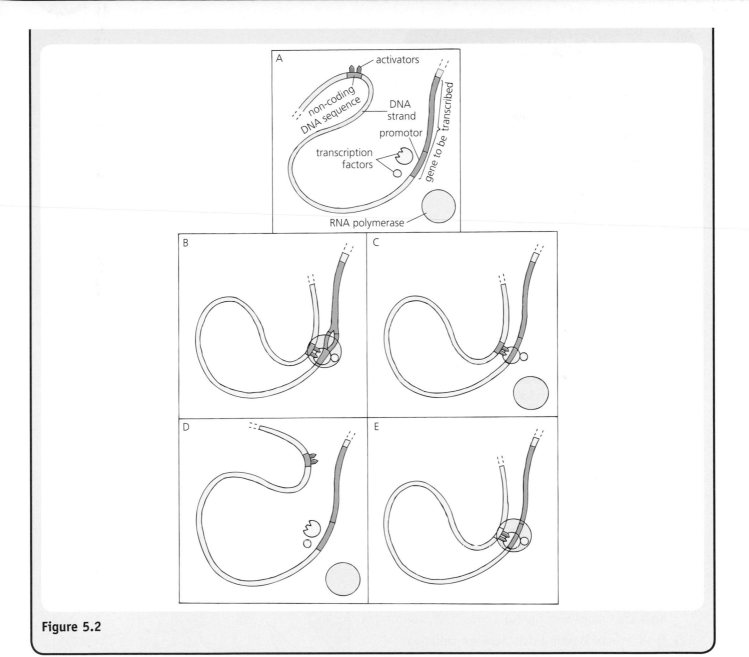

Figure 5.2

6 Mutations

1 In the following three sentences, a small error alters the sense of the message. To which type of point mutation is each of these equivalent?

a) Intended: She ordered boiled rice.

Actual: She ordered boiled ice.

b) Intended: He walked to the pillar box.

Actual: He talked to the pillar box.

c) Intended: He put a quid in his pocket.

Actual: He put a squid in his pocket. (3)

2 The data in Table 6.1 refer to the results of an experiment to investigate the effect of increasing doses of radiation on root length in germinating chick peas.

Radiation dose (units)	Mean root length (mm)
0	180
100	152
200	140
300	106
400	90
500	74
600	44

Table 6.1

a) In this experiment, which factor is the
   i) dependent variable?
   ii) independent variable? (1)

b) Plot the points on a sheet of graph paper and draw the line of best fit. (4)

c) i) What relationship exists between radiation dose and mean root length?
   ii) Suggest why. (2)

d) From your graph, extrapolate the radiation dose that would result in no root growth. (1)

e) In this experiment, ten seeds were planted per pot and four replicates of each pot were set up. Explain why. (1)

f) Although gene mutations in the absence of mutagenic agents are rare, the gene controlling grain colour in maize mutates as often as one in 2000 gametes on average. Express this as a mutation rate. (1)

3 The information in Table 6.2 refers to modern day human societies. Write a paragraph to explain the data including all of the following terms in your answer.

selective advantage, lactase-coding gene, point mutation, hunter-gatherers, early dairy farmers (5)

Human society	Post-weaning lactose tolerance (%)
European Americans	88
Native Americans (Inuit)	0
European Australians	96
Australian Aborigines	0

Table 6.2

4 a) Show diagrammatically the proportion of sufferers of sickle-cell trait that would result from a cross between
   i) a normal parent and a parent with sickle-cell trait
   ii) two parents with sickle-cell trait. (4)

b) Figure 6.1 shows a region in Africa. Each circle on the map represents the percentage of local people with sickle-cell trait. Explain the variation in incidence of sickle-cell trait in this region. (2)

5 During gamete formation, chromosomes normally form pairs that match one another, gene for gene, all along their length. The members of each pair

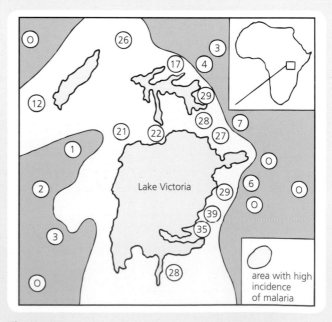

Figure 6.1

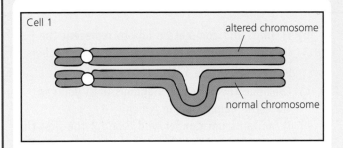

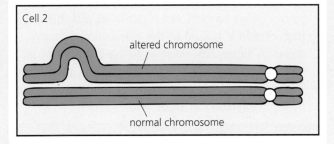

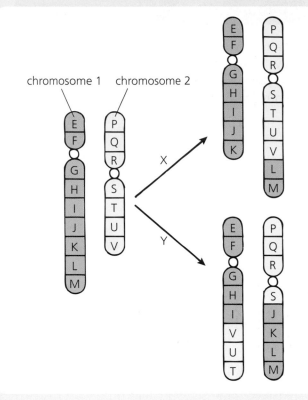

Figure 6.2

of chromosomes shown in Figure 6.2 do not match properly because of a mutation.

a) Which type of mutation has occurred in each case? (2)

b) i) Which of these would be more likely to prove lethal to the organism?
   ii) Explain your choice. (2)

6 Figure 6.3 shows two chromosomes undergoing mutations.

a) Which arrow represents
   i) reciprocal translocation?
   ii) non-reciprocal translocation? (1)

b) i) In which of these examples of translocation has an inversion also occurred?
   ii) Identify the genes that became inverted. (2)

7 Table 6.3 refers to three species of the *Brassica* group of plants.

Figure 6.3

a) Supply the answers to blank boxes **i)**, **ii)**, **iii)** and **iv)**. (2)

b) Why is the hybrid unable to make viable sex cells? (1)

c) Construct an hypothesis to explain how swede could have arisen from the sterile hybrid. (2)

d) Identify
   i) a diploid plant
   ii) a polyploid plant from the table.
   iii) Why are polyploid plants highly valued as crop plants? (3)

8 Give an account of point mutations and their impact on protein structure. (9)

Scientific name	Common name	Genomes in body cells	Genome(s) in sex cells
Brassica oleracea	cabbage	AA	**(i)**
Brassica rapa	turnip	**(ii)**	B
(not given a scientific name)	sterile hybrid between cabbage and turnip	**(iii)**	(not able to make viable sex cells)
Brassica napobrassica	swede	AABB	**(iv)**

Table 6.3

7 Evolution

1 The parents in the family tree shown in Figure 7.1 have eight children, none of whom is identical to any other with respect to the three genetically controlled traits shown.

   a) Is this form of inheritance horizontal or vertical? (1)

   b) Make a simple diagram to show the phenotypes of sons and daughters B–G. (3)

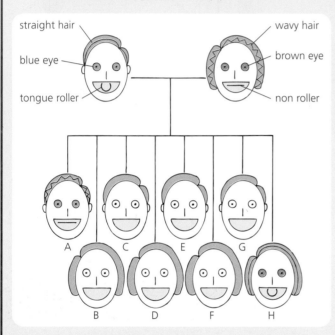

Figure 7.1

2 Figure 7.2 shows how a mutant form of a species that possesses some advantageous characteristic could spread through a population. Imagine that before dying, each mutant form leaves, on average, two offspring as part of the next generation whereas each wild type leaves only one.

   a) Which symbol represents the mutant form? (1)

   b) i) Draw and complete a box to represent the F$_2$.
      ii) State the ratio that applies to the members of its population. (2)

   c) Continue the series of diagrams until you can state the generation in which:
      i) mutants outnumber wild type for the first time
      ii) the ratio of wild type to mutants is 1:8. (2)

3 For many years, rats were successfully controlled by a poison called warfarin which interferes with the way that vitamin K is used in the biochemical pathway shown in Figure 7.3. However in 1958, strains of rat appeared in Scotland which were resistant to warfarin. This resistance is an inherited characteristic as shown by the information in Table 7.1.

Rat's genotype	Rat's phenotype
W^{s}W^s	sensitive to warfarin
W^{s}W^r	resistant to warfarin (but needs some extra vitamin K in diet)
W^{r}W^r	resistant to warfarin (but needs 20 times normal amount of vitamin K in diet)

Table 7.1

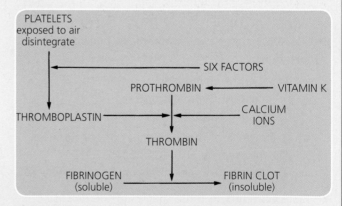

Figure 7.3

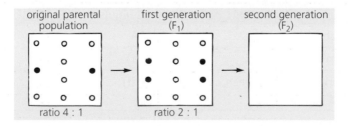

Figure 7.2

a) With reference to the diagram, explain why warfarin is lethal to normal rats. (1)

b) Why are people who suffer thrombosis (internal blood clotting) given small amounts of warfarin to take? (1)

c) Suggest how the resistant strain of rat arose. (1)

d) The resistant strain has increased greatly in number over the years. Explain this success in terms of natural selection. (1)

e) If the use of warfarin is continued, predict the fate of the normal wild type rat. (1)

f) Construct a hypothesis to account for the fact that most of the rats resistant to warfarin are heterozygotes. (2)

4 The lengths of both members of paired brine shrimps were measured to find out if their mate choice was related to body size. Table 7.2 shows the results.

a) Plot a scatter graph of the results. (4)

b) Draw a conclusion from your graph. (1)

c) i) Which mating pair had the largest combined length?
   ii) Which mating pair had the smallest combined length?

iii) Suggest why there are no data given for brine shrimps smaller than the pair you gave as the answer to ii). (3)

5 Read the passage and answer the questions that follow it.

A type of African widowbird lives in grassland. During the non-breeding season the birds are short-tailed but each year, when the mating season arrives, the males develop very long tail feathers. At this time the males also engage in contests to try to secure a territory. If successful, a male bird builds nest frames in his territory and defends it from other males.

Next he performs a flight display to show off his tail feathers and attract females to his territory. If he is chosen by a female, they mate and she lines a nest frame with grass. Then she lays and incubates her eggs in what is described as an active nest.

In an investigation, 35 male widowbirds of varying tail length were studied to find out how many active nests appeared in each bird's territory during a breeding season. Figure 7.4 shows a scatter graph of the results.

Pair number	Length of male (mm)	Length of female (mm)	Pair number	Length of male (mm)	Length of female (mm)
1	11.0	13.0	16	11.5	15.0
2	12.0	14.5	17	14.0	16.0
3	13.5	13.5	18	13.0	15.0
4	13.5	15.5	19	14.0	15.0
5	9.5	13.5	20	13.0	14.0
6	11.0	11.5	21	10.5	12.5
7	12.0	15.5	22	9.5	12.5
8	12.5	13.5	23	10.5	14.0
9	12.0	12.0	24	12.5	15.5
10	12.0	16.0	25	11.0	14.0
11	10.0	11.5	26	13.5	15.0
12	12.0	13.5	27	12.5	14.5
13	11.5	14.0	28	13.5	16.0
14	11.0	15.0	29	12.0	14.0
15	13.0	15.5	30	13.5	14.5

Table 7.2

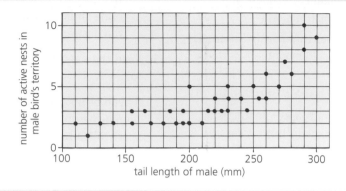

Figure 7.4

a) Why were as many as 35 male birds studied? (1)

b) What was the tail length of the
   i) most successful?
   ii) least successful bird?
   iii) In general what trend is shown by the data in the scatter graph? (3)

c) Why is sexual selection of survival value to a species? (2)

d) Which part of a widowbird's sexual selection behaviour involves
   i) male-to-male competition?
   ii) female choice? (2)

e) i) Based on the results of this investigation, predict the effect of artificially doubling the length of a male's tail to 600 mm on the number of active nests in his territory.
   ii) Give TWO possible reasons why natural selection has not selected birds that develop tails of this longer length. (3)

6 Figure 7.5 shows two possible ways in which speciation could occur.

   a) Name each type of speciation and explain your choice with reference to barriers. (4)

   b) What test could be carried out to determine if two populations of trees belonged to the same species? (2)

7 Read the passage and answer the questions that follow it.

The data in Table 7.3 and Figure 7.6 refer to three subspecies of the fieldmouse (*Apodemus sylvaticus*). Some scientists suggest that the fieldmouse became established on the Shetland Isles and Fair Isle millions of years ago while these islands were attached to the Scottish mainland. Following

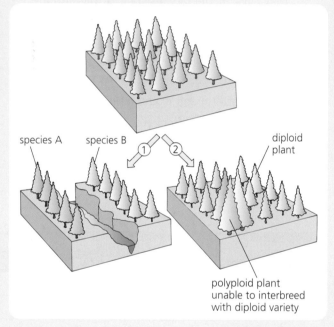

Figure 7.5

separation, each island population then took its own course of evolution.

However this theory is disputed by the work of R. J. Berry. From detailed studies of the skeletons of different subspecies of *Apodemus*, this scientist has devised a way of measuring how close or distant the relationship is between two subspecies. This is expressed as 'genetic distance' (the higher the value, the more distant the relationship).

The genetic distances of *Apodemus sylvaticus granti* and *Apodemus sylvaticus fridariensis* are given as boxed values on the map. The upper value indicates the genetic distance between the island population and the Norwegian mainland species and the lower value that between the island population and the Scottish mainland species.

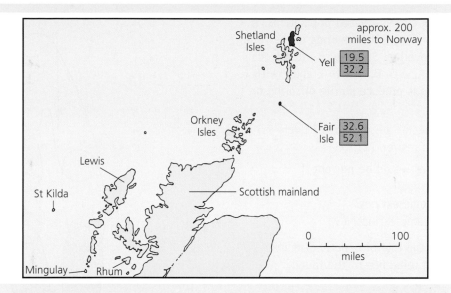

Figure 7.6

a) State ONE quantitative and ONE qualitative difference between the fieldmouse native to Fair Isle and the one from the Scottish mainland. (2)

b) Suggest why scientists do not classify the three subspecies given in Table 5.3 as separate species. (1)

c) Berry suggests that the first population of *Apodemus* became established on Yell after being brought from Norway on Viking ships. What evidence from the data supports this theory? (1)

d) i) Fossil evidence shows that *Apodemus* became extinct in Britain during the last ice age (about a million years ago). When the ice melted, the Shetland Isles became separated from the mainland and have remained so ever since. Does this information lend support to, or cast doubt on, Berry's theory?

ii) Give a reason for your answer. (2)

e) Fair Isle is thought to have been colonised by *Apodemus* from Yell. Explain the genetic distance data referring to *Apodemus sylvaticus fridariensis* in terms of the founder effect. (2)

f) St Kilda and several Hebridean Islands (such as Lewis, Mingulay and Rhum) each have their own distinct subspecies of *Apodemus*. Suggest how this could have come about. (2)

Scientific name	Location	Mean body length (mm)	Mean tail length (mm)	Ventral colour	Pectoral spot
Apodemus sylvaticus sylvaticus	Scottish mainland	92	83	dull white with slate-grey throat and belly	buff coloured area between front legs
Apodemus sylvaticus granti	Yell (Shetlands)	101	88	dull bluish-white	small spot between front legs
Apodemus sylvaticus fridariensis	Fair Isle	113	99	dull bluish-white	normally absent

Table 7.3

8 Figure 7.7 shows six closely-related populations. A and B interbreed forming fertile hybrids in the zone where their ranges overlap. Similarly B interbreeds successfully with C, C with D, D with E and E with F. All other combinations produce sterile offspring or no offspring.

a) i) How many species are present in Figure 7.7?
   ii) Explain your answer. (2)

b) How many species would be present if
   i) C became extinct?
   ii) B and D became extinct?
   iii) A and F became extinct? (3)

9 Give an account of the role of genetic drift in evolution, including reference to the founder effect. (9)

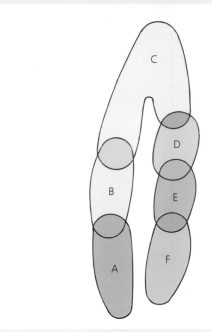

Figure 7.7

8 Genomic sequencing

1 Figure 8.1 shows the DNA fragments which resulted from two copies of part of a genome, each cut by a different restriction endonuclease. The computer found that the four larger fragments possessed overlaps.

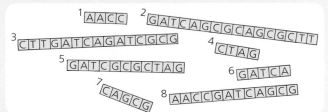

Figure 8.1

Draw a copy of these four larger fragments on squared paper, cut them out and use them to construct this part of the person's genome. (1)

2 The genetic sequences for a protein-coding gene from the genomes of two people were compared. They were found to differ by three SNPs (single nucleotide polymorphisms).

   a) Will the two people definitely differ in phenotype as a result of these differences?

   b) Explain your answer. (2)

3 Genetic material from a sample of volunteers of differing ethnic origin was collected and analysed. Table 8.1 summarises the results and shows the SNPs that occur at six closely located sites on the genome of these people. The results refer to a single strand of DNA.

   a) i) What is a single nucleotide polymorphism?
      ii) Which site in the table appears to have been least affected by SNPs? (2)

   b) By how many bases at sites 1–6 do the genomes of groups 7 and 10 differ? (1)

   c) Which group(s) has the same set of bases at these six sites in their genome as:
      i) group 1?
      ii) group 2?
      iii) group 3? (3)

   d) How many people of ethnic origin W have the same genotype as people in group 9? (1)

   e) i) Which set of six bases occurs most frequently among the total sample group?
      ii) What percentage of the total sample group possesses this set of bases in their genome? (2)

   f) Which group has the least common set of bases in its genome? (1)

   g) If the set of bases in the genome possessed by group 6 is strongly associated with a fatal disease, which other groups are at equal risk? (1)

   h) What TWO things could be done to increase the reliability of the results? (2)

Group	Ethnic origin	Number of individuals in group	Set of bases at six sites in genome as a result of SNPs					
			Site 1	Site 2	Site 3	Site 4	Site 5	Site 6
1	W	1	C	C	T	A	T	G
2	W	17	T	C	C	A	C	A
3	W	63	T	T	C	A	C	A
4	W	21	C	T	T	A	T	G
5	X	44	T	C	C	A	C	A
6	X	36	C	T	T	A	T	G
7	X	1	C	C	T	A	T	G
8	X	1	T	T	C	A	C	A
9	Y	47	T	C	C	A	C	A
10	Y	1	T	C	C	G	C	A
11	Y	87	C	T	T	A	T	G
12	Y	1	C	C	T	A	T	G

Table 8.1

4 Read the passage and answer the questions that follow it.

Two important genes

The HAR1 gene in humans is essential for the development of neurons in the growing embryo and for the formation of the cerebral cortex – a region of the brain responsible for many roles such as speech, memory, intelligence and imagination.

Chimpanzees also have the HAR1 gene. The human HAR1 gene differs from it by the possession of 18 base-pair substitutions. Chimpanzees and humans are believed to have shared a common ancestor about six million years ago. It is thought that of all the many mutations that affected the HAR1 gene over that period of time, these 18 substitutions were the ones that were retained by natural selection in humans since they led to improved human brain development.

The FOXP2 gene, located on chromosome 7 in humans, codes for FOXP2 protein which acts as a transcription factor. It plays a key role in regulating the expression of other genes such as those required for development of neural circuits in the brain and for speech.

A mutation in the FOXP2 gene in humans causes a severe speech and language disorder. Sequencing of the DNA of sufferers shows that the mutation takes the form of a substitution. This leads to one wrong amino acid being present at a crucial point on the FOXP2 protein molecule. As a result it is no longer able to regulate the genes responsible for development of the neural circuits that co-ordinate the movements that make speech possible. Chimpanzees also have the FOXP2 gene but it differs from the normal human version by two base-pair substitutions.

a) Give the word(s) from the passage that means:
   i) a nerve cell
   ii) an early type of living organism from which later dissimilar types have evolved
   iii) the general name for a change in an organism's genetic material
   iv) a regulatory protein that binds to DNA and stimulates transcription of one or more specific genes
   v) the process by which individuals best adapted to the environment survive and pass their genes on to succeeding generations. (5)

b) Humans and chimpanzees have 98.5% of their DNA in common. Give TWO examples of ways in which their DNA differs. (2)

c) Based on the information in the passage, construct an hypothesis to explain why humans are more intelligent than chimpanzees. (1)

d) Which type of mutation is referred to in the passage? (1)

e) Based on the information in the passage, construct an hypothesis to explain why chimpanzees cannot speak. (2)

f) Explain why the two genes referred to in the passage are described as being of *selective advantage* to humans. (2)

5 The graph in Figure 8.2 shows the use of cytochrome c as a molecular clock.

a) Which groups had a common ancestor until about 400 million years ago? (1)

b) i) Which groups are the most different from one another according to a comparison of their cytochrome c?
   ii) When does the fossil record suggest that they diverged? (2)

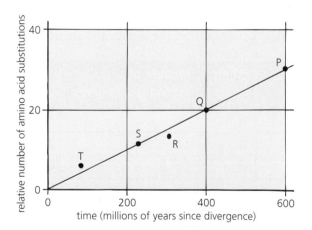

Key	comparison	groups being compared
	P	vertebrates and insects
	Q	fish and reptiles
	R	reptiles and mammals
	S	reptiles and birds
	T	two mammalian groups

Figure 8.2

c) i) Which is thought to have evolved first from a common reptilian ancestor, the birds or the mammals?
   ii) Justify your answer with molecular evidence from the graph. (2)

d) Amphibians share a common ancestor with fish. In the absence of fossil evidence, what investigation could be carried out to attempt to estimate their time of divergence using the molecular clock in Figure 8.2? (2)

6 The data in Table 8.2 refer to three micro-organisms.

   a) Calculate the values that should have been entered in boxes (i), (ii) and (iii). (3)

   b) Which micro-organism has the lowest ratio of genome length to gene number? (1)

   c) i) Which micro-organism is most likely to have the highest amount of repetitive DNA in its genome?
      ii) Explain your answer. (2)

   d) To which of the three main domains of living things does each of the three micro-organisms belong? Give ONE reason to support your choice in each case. (3)

7 a) Figure 8.3 shows a tiny part of the human genome.
   i) Imagine that the 30 base pairs shown are printed on a strip of paper that is 100 mm in length. How many metres of paper strip would be required to print out the entire human genome if it is 3 billion base pairs in length?
   ii) Convert your answer to i) into kilometres and express it as words. (2)

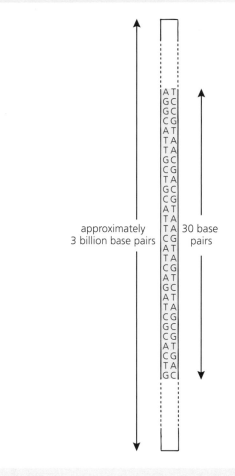

Figure 8.3

approximately 3 billion base pairs   30 base pairs

b) i) Is the human genome that was completed in 2003 likely to be an exact match for any one individual?
   ii) Explain your answer. (2)

Micro-organism	Characteristics				
	Length of genome (kb)	Number of genes that code for protein	Ratio of genome length to gene number	Relative number of introns	Nucleus with double membrane
1 Neurospora crassa	(i)	10 100	3.96 : 1	many	present
2 Bradyrhizobium japonicum	9 154.2	(ii)	1.1 : 1	none	absent
3 Methanosarcina acetivorans	5 750	4 662	(iii)	a few	absent

Note: 1 kilobase (kb) = 1×10^3 bases

Table 8.2

Alleles of gene present in genome	State of enzyme	Person's metabolic profile
	non-functional	
one null allele and one inferior allele		
		extensive
	highly functional	

Table 8.3

8 Read the passage and answer the questions that follow it.

Debrisoquine hydroxylase is an enzyme made by cells in the liver. It is responsible for the breakdown of drugs used to treat a variety of disorders such as nausea, depression and heart disorders once the drugs have brought about their desired effect.

Several alleles of the gene that codes for this enzyme occur among the members of the human population. These alleles code for different versions of the enzyme which, in turn, vary in their ability to metabolise drugs. Depending on their particular genotype, a person may produce no functional enzyme and be a poor metaboliser because both of their alleles are null and void.

If the person has one null allele and one inferior allele that code for a partly functional version of debrisoquine hydroxylase, they are said to be an intermediate metaboliser. An extensive metaboliser has one or two normal alleles which code for the fully functional form of the enzyme. Some people possess more than two copies of the normal allele and their metabolic profile is described as ultra-rapid.

a) Copy and complete Table 8.3 which summarises the passage. (4)

b) What type of mutation could account for an ultra-rapid metaboliser having more than two copies of the allele of the gene that codes for debrisoquine hydroxylase? (1)

c) i) Which group of people are most likely to be at risk of harmful side effects if given a standard dose of a drug normally broken down by debrisoquine hydroxylase?
    ii) Explain your answer. (2)

d) i) For which group of people would a standard dose of such a drug probably be ineffective?
    ii) Explain your answer. (2)

e) In what way might personalised medicine (pharmacogenetics) solve the problems referred to in questions c) and d)? (2)

Unit 2

Metabolism and Survival

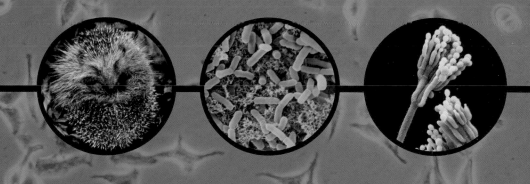

9 Metabolic pathways and their control

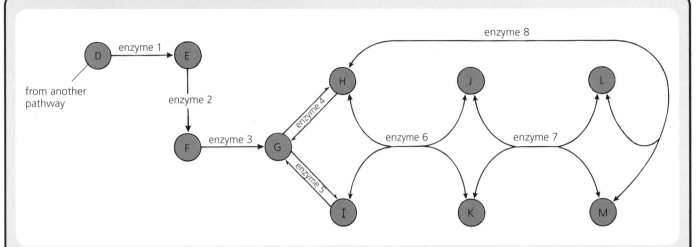

Figure 9.1

1 Figure 9.1 shows a metabolic pathway where each encircled letter represents a metabolite.

   a) How many of the reactions under enzyme control in this pathway are
   i) reversible?
   ii) irreversible? (2)

   b) Predict what would happen if metabolite I built up to a concentration far in excess of that of metabolite H. (2)

   c) i) By what alternative route could a supply of intermediates J and K be obtained if enzyme 6 becomes inactive?
   ii) By what alternative route could a supply of intermediates L and M be obtained if enzyme 8 becomes inactive?
   iii) By what alternative route could a supply of metabolite I be obtained if enzyme 5 becomes inactive? (3)

   d) Suggest a benefit to a living organism of its metabolic pathways possessing alternative routes. (1)

2 Read the passage and answer the questions that follow it.

Lysosomes are cellular organelles containing degradative enzymes which work at pH 4.5. The difference in pH between the surrounding cytoplasm (pH 7.2) and the inside of a lysosome is maintained by H^+ ions being actively pumped across the lysosome's membrane from the cytoplasm.

Lysosomes are used to digest and destroy

micro-organisms enclosed in vacuoles. They also deal with worn-out proteins from the cell surface and old and damaged organelles (see Figure 9.2). A membrane forms round a targeted organelle or piece of cellular debris to separate it from the rest of the cell in preparation for lysosomal activity. By digesting redundant structures and recycling the materials produced, the cell is able to renew itself continuously.

Some types of cells are programmed to die as a natural part of embryological development. This process is accompanied by the digestion of the entire cell by its own lysosomal enzymes. It occurs,

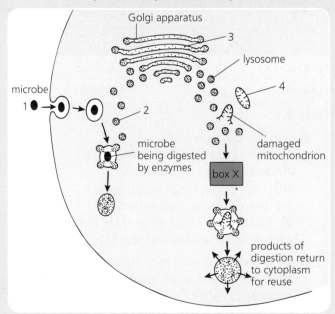

Figure 9.2

for example, in the tail cells of a tadpole as it develops into a frog.

a) Match numbered structures 1–4 in Figure 9.2 with the following descriptions:
   i) It contains a compartment of enzymes involved in energy release by aerobic respiration.
   ii) It is a flattened fluid-filled sac containing metabolites that process newly-synthesised proteins.
   iii) It is a pathogenic prokaryote.
   iv) It is a sac containing digestive enzymes that work in acidic conditions. (3)

b) Give an example of active transport from the passage and state its purpose. (2)

c) Draw a simple labelled diagram to show the stage that should have been drawn in box X. (3)

d) The hands of a normal human embryo are webbed at an early stage of development. Suggest the means by which the webbing is removed before birth. (1)

e) Suggest what happens to the molecules that previously made up a tadpole's tail cells when the animal becomes a frog. (1)

3 The data in Table 9.1 refer to ions present inside and outside muscle cells in the body of an amphibian. The graph in Figure 9.3 represents the results of an experiment set up to investigate the effect of oxygen concentration on uptake of potassium ions and consumption of sugar by muscle cells in a tissue culture.

Ion	Concentration (mmol/l)	
	Intracellular	Extracellular
potassium	137.5	2.5
sodium	13.0	104.0

Table 9.1

a) Identify the region of:
   i) high sodium concentration
   ii) low sodium concentration
   iii) high potassium concentration
   iv) low potassium concentration.
   v) Explain how these differences in ionic concentration are maintained. (3)

b) By how many times is the concentration of potassium inside a cell greater than that outside? (1)

c) i) From the graph in Figure 9.3, state the effect

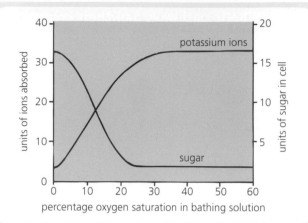

Figure 9.3

that an increase in oxygen concentration from 0–30% has on the rate of ion uptake.
   ii) Suggest why ion uptake levels off beyond 30% oxygen.
   iii) What relationship exists between units of ions absorbed and units of sugar remaining in the cell? Suggest why. (4)

4 Figure 9.4 shows the stages that occur during an enzyme-controlled reaction.

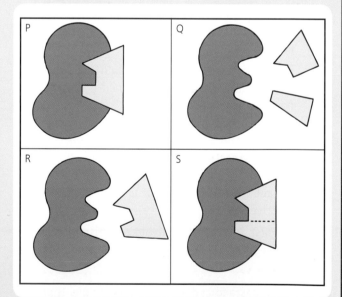

Figure 9.4

a) Which of these stages illustrates induced fit? (1)

b) Using the letters given, indicate the correct sequence in which the four stages would occur if the enzyme were promoting:
   i) the build-up of a molecule from smaller components

ii) the breakdown of a molecule into smaller constituents. (2)

5 Figure 9.5 represents, at molecular level, the effect of varying substrate concentration on the rate of an enzyme-controlled reaction.

a) Copy and complete the diagram to include the missing molecules. (3)

b) From the information in the diagram, state the factor that was kept constant by the experimenter. (1)

c) i) State the rate of the reaction in set-up 4.
ii) Why was this rate equal to that in set-up 3 despite the presence of extra substrate in 4?
iii) In which of the set-ups were active sites on enzyme molecules available since substrate molecules were in short supply? (3)

6 Give an account of enzyme activity under the headings:

a) induced fit (3)

b) activation energy (3)

c) effect of substrate concentration. (3)

7 Return to question 4 on page 30 and consider the enzyme shown in Figure 9.4. Which of the molecules shown in Figure 9.6 could act as a competitive inhibitor to this enzyme? (1)

8 Tables 9.2 and 9.3 give the results from an experiment set-up to compare the activity of an enzyme (alkaline phosphatase) with its substrate

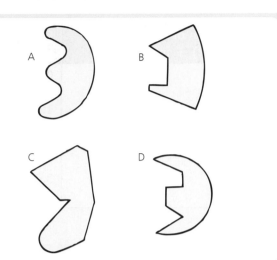

Figure 9.6

Concentration of substrate (n moles l^{-1})	Enzyme activity (units)
0	0.0
10	1.8
20	2.6
30	3.3
40	3.6
50	3.8
60	4.0
70	4.0

Table 9.2

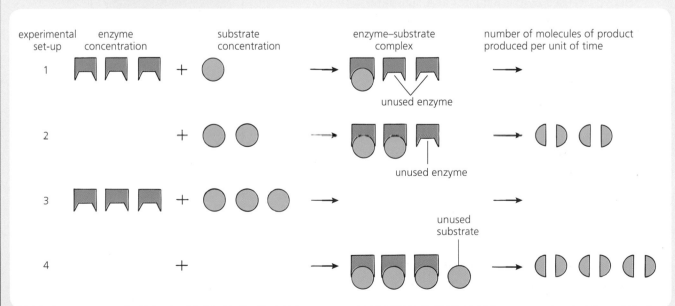

Figure 9.5

Concentration of substrate (n moles l^{-1}) + inhibitor	Enzyme activity (units)
0	0.0
10	0.6
20	1.0
30	1.5
40	2.1
50	2.7
60	3.0
70	3.6

Table 9.3

(para-nitrophenol phosphate) in the presence and absence of a competitive inhibitor.

a) i) Draw a curve of best fit for the results in Table 9.2.

ii) On the same graph, draw a line of best fit for the results in Table 9.3.

iii) Mark 'presence of inhibitor' and 'absence of inhibitor' on your graph to identify the lines. (4)

b) At which of the following ranges of substrate concentration (in n moles l^{-1}) did the enzyme activity increase at the fastest rate in the absence of inhibitor? (1)

A 0–19   **B** 20–39   **C** 40–59

c) By how many times was enzyme activity at substrate concentration of 10 n moles l^{-1} greater when the inhibitor was absent? (1)

d) Calculate the percentage decrease in enzyme activity caused by the inhibitor at a substrate concentration of:

i) 20 n moles l^{-1}

ii) 70 n moles l^{-1}. (2)

e) Why would the two lines on the graph fail to meet even if higher concentrations of substrate were used? (1)

9 Figure 9.7 refers to changes in an allosteric enzyme that controls the rate of a reaction in a metabolic pathway.

a) Match blank boxes **(i)**, **(ii)** and **(iii)** with diagrams X, Y and Z in Figure 9.8. (2)

b) Which of these lettered diagrams shows induced fit? (1)

c) Which of these lettered diagrams show an occupied allosteric site? (1)

d) Is the inhibitor that affects this enzyme *competitive* or *non-competitive*? (1)

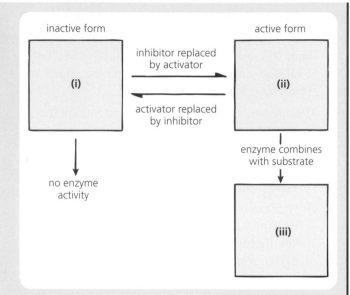

Figure 9.7

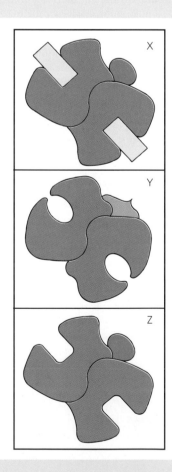

Figure 9.8

10 The experiment shown in Figure 9.9 was set up to investigate the inhibitory effect of iodine solution on the action of β-galactosidase as the concentration of the substrate ONPG was increased.

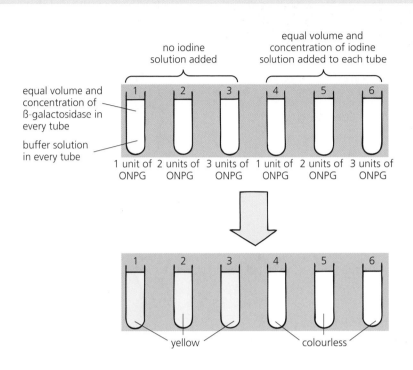

Figure 9.9

a) In which tubes did the enzyme act on its substrate? (1)

b) Identify the independent variable in this experiment. (1)

c) In which tubes was the enzyme's activity inhibited? (1)

d) Which tubes made up the experiment and which tubes were the controls? (2)

e) i) Identify the inhibitor.
   ii) Did it act competitively or non-competitively?
   iii) Explain your choice of answer. (4)

11 Figure 9.10 shows a metabolic pathway that occurs in cells of *E. coli*.

a) Identify enzyme P's
   i) substrates
   ii) products
   iii) end-product inhibitor. (3)

b) i) If there is little or no demand for cytidylic acid for use in other metabolic pathways, what effect will this have on the concentration of carbamyl phosphate?
   ii) Explain your answer. (2)

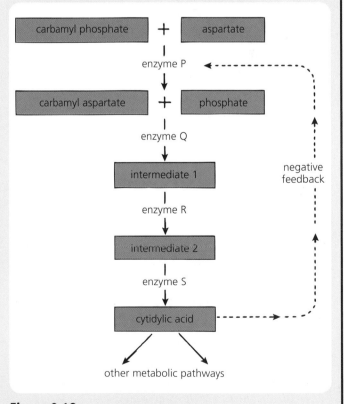

Figure 9.10

c) i) If there is a high demand for cytidylic acid in other metabolic pathways, will the negative feedback process be increased or decreased?

   ii) Explain your answer. (2)

d) Which of the following statements is/are true? (1)

   1 The end product inhibits an early step in its own synthesis.

   2 The negative feedback mechanism regulates the rate of synthesis of metabolic intermediates.

   3 End-product inhibition prevents the build-up of intermediates which would be wasteful to the cell.

12 Give an account of the control of metabolic pathways by the regulation of enzyme action. (9)

10 Cellular respiration

1 Metabolism falls into two parts:
- **anabolism** consisting of energy-requiring reactions which involve synthesis of complex molecules
- **catabolism** consisting of energy-yielding reactions in which complex molecules are broken down.

Transfer of energy from catabolic reactions to anabolic reactions is brought about by **ATP**.

Figure 10.1 is a summary of this information.

a) Copy the diagram and add four arrowheads to show the directions in which the two coupled reactions occur. (2)

b) Complete boxes 1–4 using each of the terms given in purple bold print in the passage. (2)

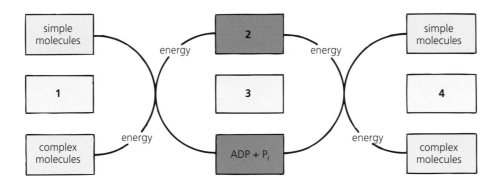

Figure 10.1

2 State whether each of the following is an anabolic (A) or a catabolic (C) reaction:

a) destruction of a microbe by enzymes in lysosomes

b) formation of the hormone thyroxin in the thyroid gland

c) conversion of glycogen to glucose in muscle tissue

d) digestion of proteins to amino acids

e) synthesis of nucleic acids. (5)

3 One mole of glucose releases 2880 kJ of energy. During aerobic respiration in living organisms, 44% of this is used to generate ATP. The rest is lost as heat.

a) What percentage of the energy generated during aerobic respiration is lost as heat? (1)

b) Out of a mole of glucose, how many kilojoules are used to generate ATP? (1)

c) Name TWO forms of cellular work that the energy held by ATP could be used to carry out. (2)

4 Table 10.1 refers to the process of cellular respiration in the presence of oxygen.

a) Copy the table and complete the blanks indicated by brackets. (5)

b) Which stage consists of an energy investment phase followed by an energy pay-off phase? (1)

c) At which stage is *most* ATP produced per molecule of glucose? (1)

d) At which TWO stages do the end products of fat digestion enter the pathway? (2)

e) Which TWO stages would fail to occur in the absence of oxygen? (2)

Stage of respiratory pathway	Principal reaction or process that occurs	Products
glycolysis	splitting of glucose into [_____]	[_____], NADH and pyruvate
[_____] acid cycle	removal of [_____] ions from molecules of respiratory [_____]	[_____], FADH$_2$, [_____] and ATP
[_____] transport chain	release of [_____] to form ATP	ATP and [_____]

Table 10.1

5 Figure 10.2 shows a small region of an inner mitochondrial membrane.

   a) i) Which side of the membrane has the higher concentration of H⁺ ions?

   ii) Explain how this higher concentration of H⁺ ions is maintained. (3)

   b) i) Name molecule X.

   ii) Briefly describe how it works. (3)

   c) Cyanide is a chemical that binds with the electron transport chains and brings the flow of high-energy electrons to a halt. Explain why cyanide is poisonous? (2)

6 Figure 10.3 shows, in a simple way, the molecular structure of three types of sugar.

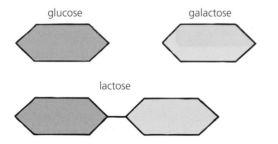

Figure 10.3

Table 10.2 shows the results of an investigation into the use by yeast of each of these sugars as its respiratory substrate.

   a) Draw a line graph of the results on the same sheet of graph paper using three different colours. (4)

   b) i) Identify the glucose result that was least reliable.

   ii) Justify your choice. (2)

Time (min)	Total volume of carbon dioxide released (ml)		
	Glucose	Galactose	Lactose
0	0.0	0.0	0.0
10	0.0	0.0	0.0
20	0.5	0.0	0.0
30	3.0	0.5	0.5
40	6.0	1.0	0.5
50	11.0	1.5	1.5
60	16.0	1.5	1.5
70	18.0	2.0	2.0
80	32.5	2.0	2.5
90	39.5	2.0	3.0

Table 10.2

   c) What percentage increase in total volume of carbon dioxide released occurred for glucose between 20 minutes and 80 minutes? (1)

   d) What conclusion can be drawn about yeast's ability to make use of each of the sugars as its respiratory substrate? (1)

   e) i) What conclusion can be drawn about yeast's ability to break lactose down into its component sugars within the given time span?

   ii) Explain your answer. (2)

   f) What could be done to improve the reliability of the results? (1)

   g) Predict what the outcome would have been if the enzyme β-galactosidase had been added to each flask at the start of the experiment. (2)

7 Figure 10.4 shows a simplified version of several interconnecting metabolic pathways that occur in the human body.

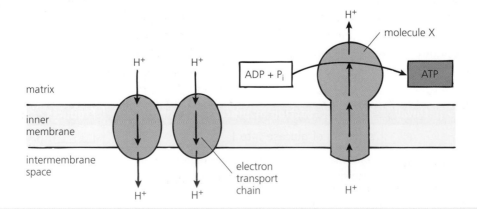

Figure 10.2

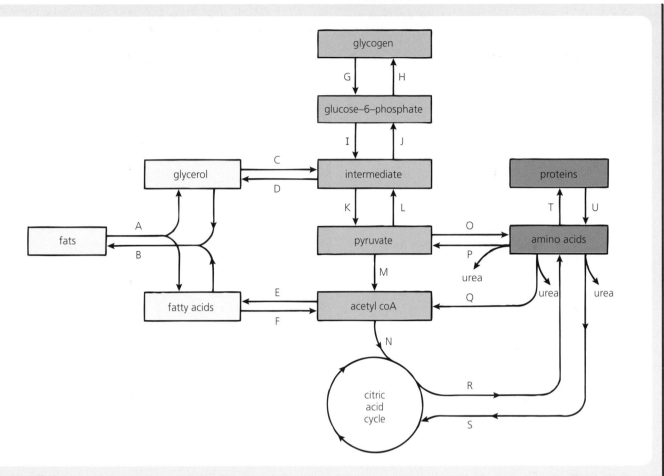

Figure 10.4

Questions **a)** and **b)** below both refer to the following four possible answers:

  A B, E, M, P, U
  B G, I, K, M, N
  C A, E, N, R, Q
  D K, M, N, R, T

a) Which route would result in the synthesis of a complex molecule needed for tissue repair? (1)

b) Which route would lead on to the generation of much ATP by electron transport chains? (1)

c) **i)** Can a person build up and store fat if they consume excessive quantities of fat-free food over a long period?
  ii) Explain your answer with reference to Figure 10.4. (3)

d) How is it possible that a person can survive for many days without food? (2)

8 Figure 10.5 shows the volume of carbon dioxide released by yeast cells during the fermentation of glucose.

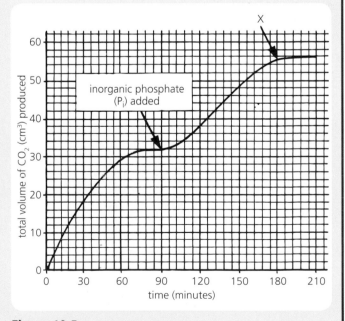

Figure 10.5

a) For which specific biochemical process does a yeast cell require a supply of inorganic phosphate (P_i)? (1)

b) Inorganic phosphate was added at 90 minutes. Name the substance to which it became combined. (1)

c) i) State what happened to the rate of carbon dioxide production following the addition of inorganic phosphate at 90 minutes.

ii) Suggest a reason for this change. (2)

d) Give a possible explanation for the levelling off of carbon dioxide production at point X on the graph. (1)

11 Metabolic rate

1 The graph in Figure 11.1 shows basal metabolic rate for humans aged 1–70 years.

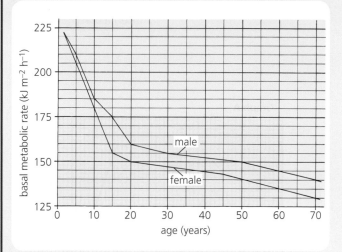

Figure 11.1

a) Draw TWO conclusions from the graph. (2)

b) By how many times is the basal metabolic rate (BMR) of a 5-year-old male greater than that of a 70-year-old male? (1)

c) What percentage decrease in BMR occurs in females between the ages of 10 and 70 years? (1)

2 a) Calculate the total surface area and the total volume of the cube shown in Figure 11.2
   i) before it was sawn up
   ii) after it was sawn up. (2)

b) Calculate the surface area to volume ratio of
   i) the original large cube
   ii) one of the smaller cubes produced after cutting. (2)

c) Imagine that each size of cube represents a living organism. Which size would tend to lose more heat relative to its body size when the external temperature is low? (1)

d) Figure 11.3 refers to six species of shrew. Which species has:
   i) the smallest body size?
   ii) the largest body size? (1)

e) Which species of shrew has:
   i) the lowest metabolic rate?
   ii) the highest metabolic rate? (1)

f) i) What is the overall relationship between body size and metabolic rate?

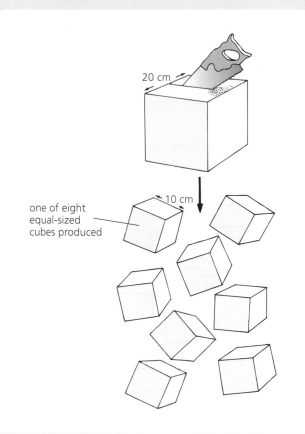

Figure 11.2

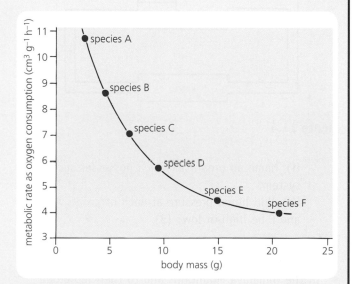

Figure 11.3

ii) Relate your answer to i) to your answer to part c). (2)

Vertebrate group	Type of circulation	Number of chambers in heart	Pressure of blood arriving at skeletal muscles	Evolutionary level of circulatory system
fish				
	incomplete double			intermediate
mammal				

Table 11.1

3 **a)** Copy and complete Table 11.1. (5)

   b) i) Which type of circulatory system is shown in Figure 11.4?

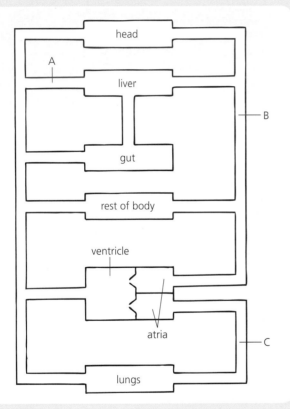

Figure 11.4

   ii) Name an organism which possesses such a system.
   iii) Will blood pressure at each of points A, B and C be high or low? (5)

4 Graphs A and B in Figure 11.5 refer to the altitudes reached by a group of climbers on an expedition in the Himalaya Mountains and to their red blood corpuscle (cell) counts.

   a) State the climbers':
   i) starting altitude
   ii) altitude after 40 days. (2)

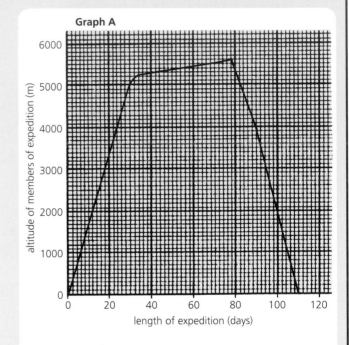

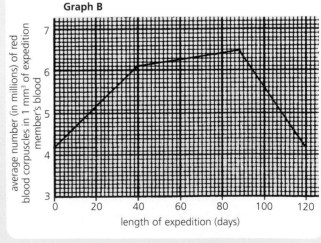

Figure 11.5

   b) How many million red corpuscles per mm^3 were, on average, present in a climber's blood:
   i) at the start of the expedition?
   ii) after 40 days? (2)

   c) i) On which day did the climbers reach the highest altitude?

ii) What was the average number of red corpuscles per mm³ present in a climber's blood on this day? (2)

d) i) In general, what relationship exists between the two graphs?
ii) Explain why such a relationship is necessary for survival. (2)

e) How long did the members of the expedition spend at an altitude of 4000 m or above? (1)

f) i) Which one of the graphs lags slightly behind the other?
ii) Suggest why. (2)

g) Some athletes train for several weeks in high-altitude locations. Why might this give them a competitive advantage when they compete in events at sea level? (2)

12 Metabolism in conformers and regulators

1 *Anolis cristatellus* is a lizard that lives in open lowlands and dense forests in Puerto Rico. The graph in Figure 12.1 shows the relationship between mean body temperature and mean external air temperature for two populations. Members of population X often move to nearby sunny spots and bask in sunshine; members of population Y almost never seek out sunny spots (which are rare in the dense forest).

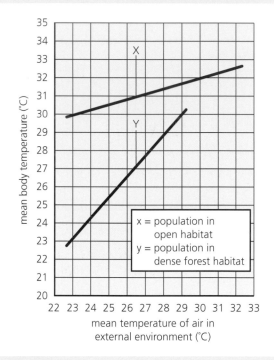

Figure 12.1

a) What is the mean body temperature of a lizard from population X when the external temperature is
   i) 23°C?
   ii) 30°C? (1)

b) What is the mean body temperature of a lizard from population Y when the external temperature is
   i) 23°C?
   ii) 30°C? (1)

c) Which animal's body is
   i) completely dependent on external temperature?
   ii) partly independent of external temperature? (1)

d) i) Which animal is not a complete conformer?
   ii) Does this animal regulate its body temperature by physiological or behavioural means? (2)

e) Suggest TWO possible reasons why members of population Y rarely move to find a sunny spot when they feel cold. (2)

2 Figure 12.2 represents a section through human skin.

a) Name the part of the brain to which heat and cold receptors relay information about the external environment. (1)

b) By what means does the thermoregulatory centre of the brain communicate information to structures X and Y in order to affect control of body temperature? (1)

c) i) In what way should structure X respond following a drop in body temperature?
   ii) Explain how this response would help to conserve heat. (2)

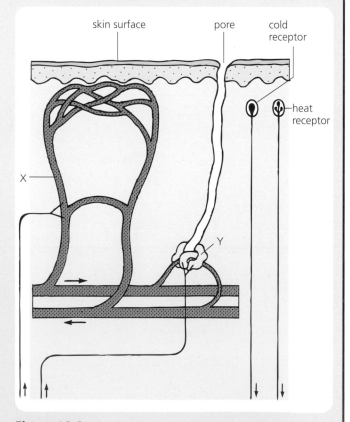

Figure 12.2

d) i) In what way would structure Y respond to an increase in body temperature?
ii) Explain how this response would help to promote heat loss. (2)

3 The data in Table 12.1 refer to the body temperature of a student who exercised vigorously and then, after a rest, plunged into a cold bath. Body temperature was measured every 2 minutes by inserting a sterilised thermistor under the student's tongue.

Time (minutes)	Body temperature (°C)
0	37.00
2	37.00
4	37.00
6	37.05
8	37.10
10	37.10
12	37.15
14	37.20
16	37.30
18	37.40
20	37.50
22	37.60
24	37.60
26	37.50
28	37.45
30	37.40
32	37.40
34	37.35
36	37.35
38	36.90
40	36.65
42	36.70
44	36.80
46	36.85
48	37.00
50	37.00

Table 12.1

a) Plot a line graph of the data. (3)
b) Using FOUR arrows, indicate on your graph that:
i) exercise was begun at minute 2
ii) exercise was stopped at minute 22
iii) immersion in the cold bath occurred at minute 34
iv) exit from the cold bath took place at minute 40. (4)

c) In general what trend in body temperature occurs during:
i) the period of vigorous exercise?
ii) the time in the cold bath?
iii) Why is there a slight delay before each of these trends begins? (3)

d) The student's skin was flushed from minute 18 onwards.
i) Suggest why.
ii) What is the benefit to the body of flushed skin? (2)

e) i) At which ONE of the following times in minutes was the student found to be shivering?

A 2   **B** 22   **C** 32   **D** 42
ii) What is the survival value of shivering? (2)

4 Write an essay on negative feedback control in the human body with reference to control of body temperature. (9)

13 Metabolism and adverse conditions

1 Figure 13.1 shows a flow diagram of the steps involved in conserving the seeds of a rare plant in a seed bank. It failed its germination test after ten years of storage.

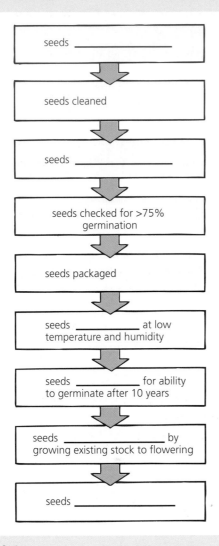

Figure 13.1

a) Copy and complete the diagram using the following answers:

stored, dried, regenerated, collected, re-stored, tested (5)

b) What evidence would have indicated that the seeds were still viable after 10 years? (1)

c) Describe the conditions maintained in a seed bank to store seeds. (2)

2 The data in Table 13.1 refer to marmots (a type of European rodent) that hibernate in winter.

Bodily function	State of animal	
	Active	Hibernating
basal metabolic rate (kJ m^{-2} day^{-1})	1728	113
body temperature (°C)	36	3
breathing rate (breaths min^{-1})	26.0	0.2
heart rate (beats min^{-1})	80	5

Table 13.1

a) By how many times does heart rate decrease during hibernation? (1)

b) What would be the basal metabolic rate per *minute* in active marmots? (1)

c) By how many times does the breathing rate increase when the animal becomes active in spring? (1)

d) What percentage decrease in body temperature occurs during hibernation? (1)

3 A tomato seed is surrounded by a capsule of juicy 'gel' which can be removed from the seed by careful washing and use of a strainer. In an experiment at a seed bank, seeds from a rare variety of tomato from South America were arranged in a Petri dish as shown in Figure 13.2 and incubated at the optimum temperature for their germination.

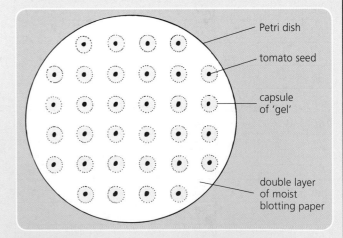

Figure 13.2

a) This experiment was set up to investigate the hypothesis that the juicy gel contains a chemical that keeps the seeds dormant. What result would support this hypothesis? (1)

b) What control should have been set up? (1)

c) What should have been done to increase the reliability of the results? (1)

d) By what means could the experiment be extended to investigate whether the juicy gel present in tomatoes grown in Scotland contains a chemical that keeps the South American seeds dormant? (3)

e) When valuable seeds arrive at a seed bank, a sample of them is tested to ensure that at least 75% of the seeds germinate if given suitable conditions.
   i) If none of the seeds germinate what further treatment should be tried before discarding the seeds?
   ii) Explain your answer. (2)

4 Read the passage and answer the questions that follow it.

The European hedgehog lives in wooded areas; the desert hedgehog lives at the edge of the Sahara desert. The European hedgehog eats earthworms and insects but these become unavailable in very cold weather. It hibernates to survive harsh winter conditions and scarcity of food. Its metabolic rate drops to a minimum, its body temperature decreases to 6 °C, its heart rate drops from 100 to 10 beats min^{-1} and its breathing rate decreases significantly. Like other deep hibernators, it may awaken a few times to feed although some individuals sleep throughout the whole hibernation period.

The desert hedgehog eats scorpions and snakes but these go deep underground when the desert becomes intolerably hot in summer. It is then that the desert hedgehog retreats to a burrow and enters a state of aestivation. Its metabolic rate slows down but not to nearly as low a level as that shown by the European hedgehog during hibernation. If the desert were to get as cold as an extreme European winter, the desert hedgehog would die because it is unable to go into deep hibernation. Even in aestivation, it only sleeps for about a week at a time and may make brief visits outside the burrow before returning to sleep.

a) Construct a table to show FIVE differences between the two types of hedgehog based on the information in the passage. (5)

b) Compared to European hedgehogs, desert hedgehogs have smaller bodies and larger pinnae (ear flaps). Suggest why. (2)

c) Brown fat cells are larger and contain more fat droplets than normal white fat cells.
   i) Suggest which type of hedgehog has a layer of brown fat cells under the skin around its neck and shoulders.
   ii) Justify your choice of answer. (3)

5 Read the passage and answer the questions that follow it.

Bird ringing normally involves placing a metal band (ring) around a bird's right leg. To trap nocturnal migrants, fine nylon netting is erected at sunset between upright poles at a trapping site chosen by ornithologists who are already familiar with the flight routes of the birds. Successful trapping is indicated later in the night by shrill cries of distress. Each trapped bird has to be carefully held round the body (not the wings or head), freed from the netting and placed in a cotton bag.

Back in the laboratory at the research base, the bird is checked for rings, coloured marks and flags and then its details (such as species and body measurements) are recorded. If it does not have a band, it is fitted with one of a size appropriate to its species before being released. This band, bearing engraved information, is secured to the bird using special pliers and the information added to the database.

a) The following list gives some of the events involved in ringing a bird. Arrange them into the correct order. (1)

   A release bird from netting

   B fit appropriate band

   C choose trapping site

   D transfer bird in bag to research base

   E release bird from research base

   F erect nylon netting

   G record bird's details

   H listen for trapped birds.

b) Describe how an ornithologist would band a trapped bird without harming it. (3)

c) What information is obtained from banded birds? (1)

6 The brambling is a bird which overwinters in Britain and then migrates north to its Scandinavian breeding area in spring. Normally it is active during the day and inactive at night. However it is found

→

to become active at night just before migration. This behaviour is known to be triggered by changes in photoperiod. The graph in Figure 13.3 shows the results from a series of experiments on the brambling. Table 13.2 gives details of natural day lengths.

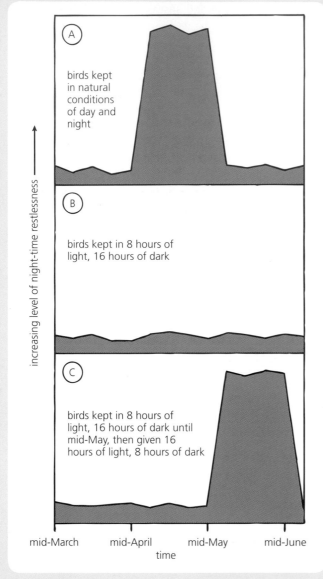

Figure 13.3

a) What happens to day length as the season changes from spring to summer? (1)

b) i) Give precise details of the environmental stimulus that triggers night-time restlessness.
ii) When does this occur under natural conditions? (2)

c) Suggest why group C failed to show night-time restlessness until mid-May. (1)

d) A pupil studied the data and concluded that the critical environmental stimulus was ten or more hours of darkness. Explain why the data do not support this conclusion. (1)

7 Figure 13.4 shows the results of an experiment carried out on a species of bird that normally migrates in autumn from Sweden to Spain. The birds were captured at point X in Holland and released at point Y in Eastern Europe.

a) Which arrow represents the displacement route? (1)

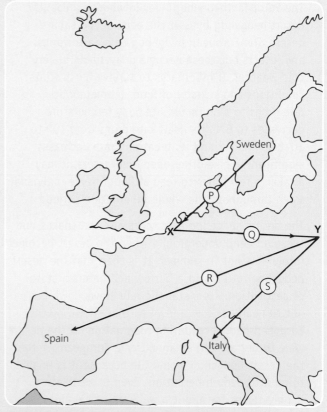

Figure 13.4

	Mid-March	Mid-April	Mid-May	Mid-June
Length of day (h)	12	14	15.5	16.5
Length of night (h)	12	10	8.5	7.5

Table 13.2

b) **i)** Is innate behaviour inherited or learned by trial and error?

ii) Which arrows represent migration that could be achieved by innate behaviour alone? (2)

c) Which arrow represents migration by displaced birds based on both innate behaviour and knowledge gained from previous experience? (1)

d) Suggest why some birds failed to reach the correct destination in Spain and arrived in Italy instead. (2)

8 Table 13.3 refers to four genera of green sulphur bacteria. Construct a key of paired statements that could be used to identify each genus quickly. (3)

9 Give an account of the specialised techniques employed in studies of long-distance migration by vertebrates and invertebrates. (9)

Genus	Cell shape	Cell arrangement	Motile?	Vacuoles present?
Chlorobium	rod-shaped	single or as short chains	no	no
Prosthecochloris	egg-shaped	single or as short chains	no	no
Clathrochloris	rod-shaped	long chains	yes	no
Pelodictyon	rod-shaped	long chains	no	yes

Table 13.3

14 Environmental control of metabolism

1 Figure 14.1 shows the tip of a growing thread of a filamentous fungus.

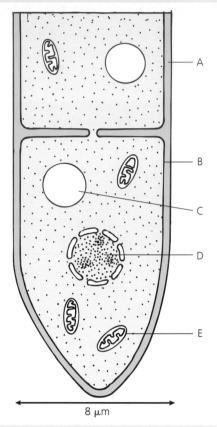

Figure 14.1

a) Name parts A–E. (5)

b) Rewrite the following sentence choosing the correct answer at each choice.

This filamentous fungus is a unicellular/multicellular member of the eukaryotes/prokaryotes. (2)

c) Express the width of this type of fungal thread in:

i) millimetres

ii) metres. (2)

2 a) Which part of Figure 14.2 shows a fermenter correctly set up and ready for use? (1)

b) With reference to the diagram, give ONE reason why each of the others is not correctly set up. (3)

3 The graph in Figure 14.3 (see page 50) shows the results from closely monitoring the changes that took place during the fermentation of a closed batch of wine.

a) i) Which line represents the number of live yeast cells?

ii) Justify your choice of answer. (2)

b) i) Which line represents the mass of glucose present in the fermenter?

ii) Justify your choice of answer. (2)

c) i) Which line represents the mass of alcohol present in the fermenter?

ii) Justify your choice of answer. (2)

4 An inoculum of 3×10^3 bacteria was added to nutrient medium in a fermenter and given optimum conditions for growth. The bacterium's doubling time was 20 minutes.

a) Copy and complete Table 14.1. (4)

Time (in 20-minute intervals)	Cell number ($\times 10^3$)	Cell number (correct to two decimal places)
0	3	3.00×10^3
1	6	
2	12	1.20×10^4
3	24	2.40×10^4
4	48	
5		
6		1.92×10^5
7		
8	768	7.68×10^5
9		
10		
11	6 144	6.14×10^6
12		

Table 14.1

b) How long did it take for the bacterial population to exceed 3 million? (1)

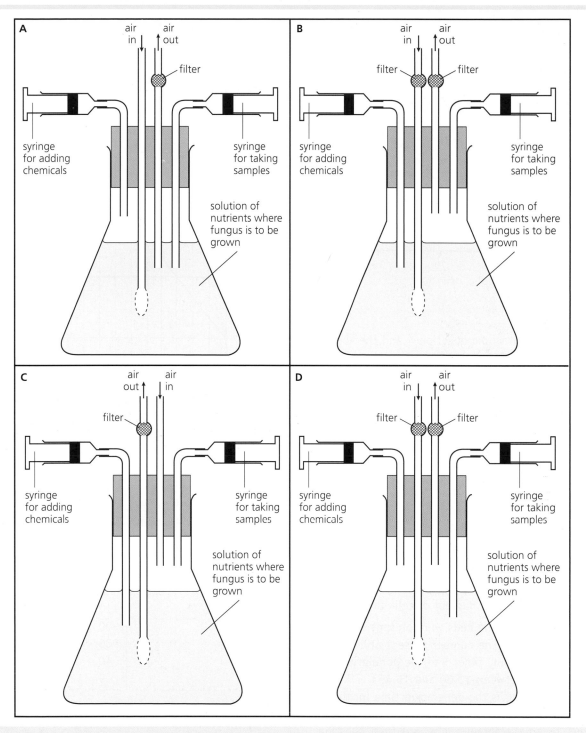

Figure 14.2

5 The time taken by a generation of micro-organisms to divide and double in number is called the mean generation time.

If **p** = number of bacteria at the start,

  q = number of bacteria after **n** generations,

n = number of generations,

g = mean generation time (min)

and **t** = time for **n** generations (min),

then $q = p \times 2^n$ and $g = t/n$.

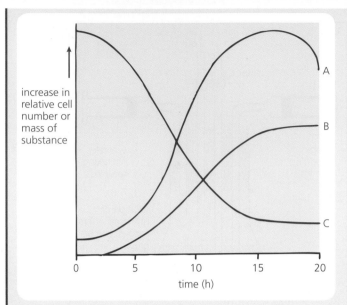

Figure 14.3

a) Using the data from question 4 and the above formulae, confirm that after 1 hour:
   i) the bacterial population should be 24 000
   ii) the generation time is 20 minutes. (Show your working.) (2)

b) Calculate the mean generation time for a colony of bacteria which began as a population of 1000 and had grown to a population of 16×10^3 after 2 hours. (Show your working.) (2)

6 The graph in Figure 14.4 shows the log phase of growth of a species of bacterium.

   a) What values should have been entered at points P and Q on the y-axis scale? (2)

   b) i) How many cells were present at time 14.15?
      ii) Now state this number of cells in words. (2)

   c) i) How many more cells were present at 15.00 compared with the number present at 12.45?
      ii) By how many times had the population multiplied between 12.00 and 15.45?
      iii) How long is the generation time for this micro-organism?
      iv) Using the formula $g = t/n$ from question 5, confirm your answer to **iii)**. (Show your working.) (4)

7 Table 14.2 shows the results of growing a batch culture of bacteria.

   a) Using a sheet of semi-log graph paper similar to the one shown in Figure 14.5, draw a line graph of the results by plotting the points and joining them together with straight lines. (4)

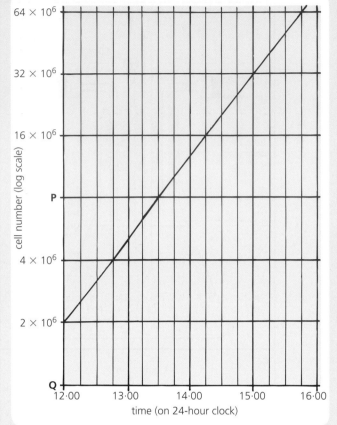

Figure 14.4

Time on 24-hour clock	Number of viable cells ($\times 10^6$)
08.00	2
10.00	2
12.00	3
14.00	8
18.00	110
22.00	900
08.00	900
12.00	40
14.00	9

Table 14.2

   b) On your graph indicate clearly:
      i) the exponential phase of growth
      ii) the death phase. (2)

   c) For how many hours was the experiment run? (1)

   d) i) When drawing a conclusion from these data, which part of the graph is least reliable?
      ii) Explain your answer.
      iii) What could be done in a repeat of the experiment to make this part of the graph more reliable? (3)

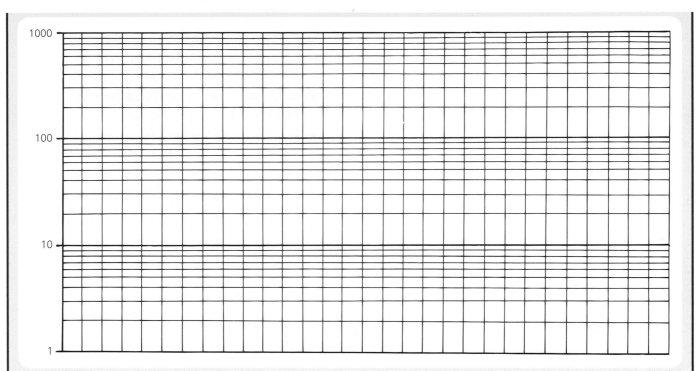

Figure 14.5

8 Read the passage and answer the questions that follow it.

Industrial production of citric acid (citrate)

Citric acid is a most useful chemical. It plays important roles in the cleaning of metals and in electroplating. However, it is probably better known for its extensive use in the food industry where its addition to many drinks and foodstuffs gives them a tart (acidic) flavour. In the past citric acid was obtained from the juice of citrus fruits such as lemons. Nowadays it is produced industrially using the filamentous fungus *Aspergillus niger*, yeast or certain types of bacteria in a submerged fermentation process.

The formation of citric acid needs both glycolysis and the start of the citric acid cycle (see Figure 14.6) to take place within the cells of the respiring micro-organism. However, to make citrate accumulate, scientists had to find a way of preventing its metabolism from continuing on round the citric acid cycle. This was achieved by removing iron (which activates the next enzyme in the cycle) from the growth medium (see Figure 14.7).

The scientists were concerned that if the cycle was brought to a halt, there would be no production of oxaloacetate needed for the formation of citric acid.

However, formation of oxaloacetate was found to continue by the opening up of a different pathway in the cell's metabolism (see Figure 14.7).

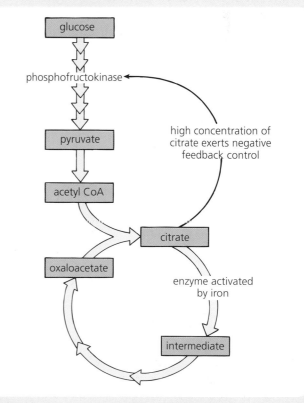

Figure 14.6

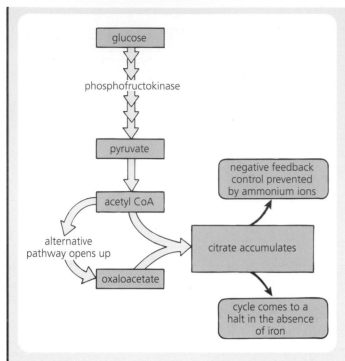

Figure 14.7

The next problem was to prevent the high concentrations of citric acid that accumulated exerting negative feedback control by inhibiting the action of the enzyme phosphofructokinase during glycolysis. This problem was overcome by using ammonium salts in the growth medium. Ammonium ions counteract the inhibitory effect of citrate (see Figure 14.7).

When *Aspergillus niger* is used, the fermentation must be highly aerated, maintained at 30 °C and at a low pH. Under these conditions the process can produce a citric acid yield of up to 18.0 kg/m³/day.

a) State THREE uses of citric acid given in the passage. (1)

b) i) What THREE problems did scientists think they would need to overcome to produce industrial quantities of citric acid?
ii) Explain why one of these did not turn out to be a problem.
iii) By what chemical means were the other two problems solved? (6)

c) i) What phrase in the passage suggests that *Aspergillus niger* is an obligate aerobe?
ii) Explain your answer. (2)

d) Suggest why the fermenter must be kept at 30 °C. (1)

e) Which chemical element essential for protein synthesis is present in ammonium salts? (1)

f) i) Convert the yield of citric acid given in the passage into grams per cubic metre per minute.
ii) Express your answer to i) using symbols and negative indices where appropriate but *without* the use of a forward slash or the word *per*. (2)

9 Give an account of the four phases of growth undergone by a population of bacteria growing in a finite volume of liquid culture medium. (9)

15 Genetic control of metabolism

1 The graph in Figure 15.1 shows the results and the line of best fit for three versions of the same experiment on bacteria carried out by three different scientific teams A, B and C.

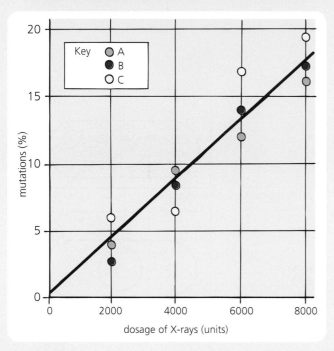

Figure 15.1

a) Identify the
   i) dependent variable
   ii) independent variable. (2)

b) What conclusion can be drawn from the results? (1)

c) Which team's set of data:
   i) deviates to the greatest extent from the line of best fit?
   ii) deviates to the least extent from the line of best fit? (2)

d) Suggest why site-specific mutagenesis is normally a preferable method of strain improvement than exposure of a culture of the organism to a mutagen such as X-rays. (2)

e) The mutation frequency of a bacterium can be expressed as the number of mutations that occur at a genetic site per million cells. In the pneumonia bacterium, it is estimated that the gene for resistance to penicillin arises spontaneously in 1 in 10^7 cells. Express this as a mutation frequency. (1)

2 Figure 15.2 shows a strain improvement breeding plan for a species of micro-organism.

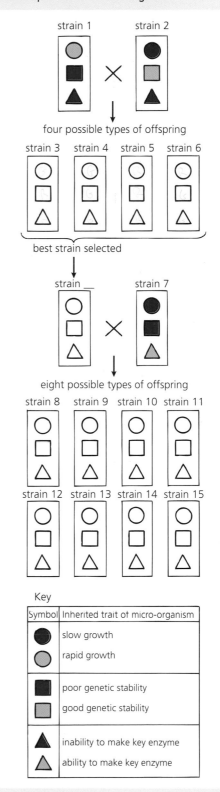

Figure 15.2

The key shows the symbols used to represent the inherited traits being selected for or against.

a) Using the same red/green colour code, copy and complete the diagram. (4)

b) On your diagram, use a large tick to indicate the very best strain. (1)

3 Figure 15.3 shows a sequence of events involving a cell of *E. coli* and a bacteriophage (phage) virus.

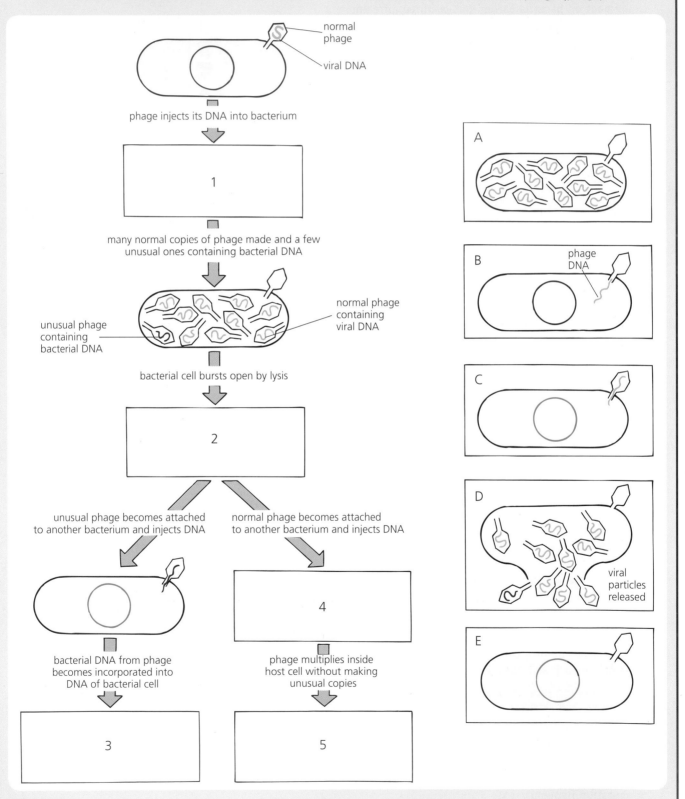

Figure 15.3

a) Match diagrams A–E with blank boxes 1–5. (4)

b) Which of diagrams A–E shows a bacterium that contains recombinant DNA? (1)

c) A bacterium containing recombinant DNA can also arise by the process of transformation.
i) Explain how transformation differs from the process shown in Figure 15.3.
ii) Is transformation an example of horizontal or vertical inheritance? (3)

4 The following list gives the steps employed during recombinant DNA technology.

A Host cell allowed to multiply.

B Required section of DNA cut out of appropriate chromosome.

C Duplicated plasmids allowed to express a 'foreign' gene.

D Plasmid extracted from bacterium and opened up.

E Recombinant plasmid inserted into the bacterial host cell.

F DNA section sealed into plasmid.

a) Arrange the steps into the correct order. (1)

b) i) During which stages would a restriction endonuclease be employed?
ii) Why would the same one need to be used for both stages? (3)

c) During which stage(s) would ligase be used? (1)

5 Strains of yeast containing recombinant DNA for insulin, but with one or more codons for certain amino acids altered, have been used to make 'insulin analogues'. A chemical analogue is a substance that mimics another substance. Some insulin analogues act more rapidly than original biosynthetic insulin because they are more readily absorbed from the injection site. The activity of two insulin analogues, X and Y, is shown in Figure 15.4.

a) Identify from the graph:
i) the prolonged-action analogue
ii) the rapid-acting analogue. (1)

b) i) For how long does the rapid-acting analogue continue to act?
ii) When does it have its maximum effect? (1)

c) For how many hours does the prolonged-action analogue continue to act at its maximum level? (1)

d) Suggest why the use of a combination of X and Y is more effective than the use of original biosynthetic insulin on its own. (2)

6 Give an account of the use of plasmids in recombinant DNA technology and describe the features that a recombinant plasmid must possess in order to carry out its role. (10)

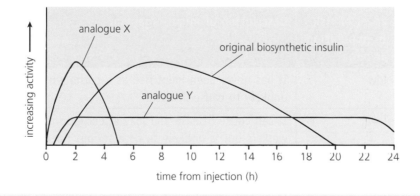

Figure 15.4

16 Ethical considerations in the use of microorganisms

1 Read the passage and answer the questions that follow it.

Clinical trials of a new drug

A large pharmaceutical company designed a new drug, Q, to treat moderate-to-severe allergic asthma in sufferers whose condition was barely or inadequately controlled by inhaled corticosteroids. During the development process, the company ran a series of clinical trials.

Phase I involved trying out drug Q on a large number of healthy volunteers who received financial incentives. In phase II, Q was administered to a few unpaid asthma sufferers who continued to use their inhalers when necessary. Phase III took the form of a trial involving 1000 asthma sufferers who continued to inhale corticosteroids as required. Half received drug Q and half received a placebo.

The results of phase III showed that patients treated with Q over a 48-week period suffered significantly fewer asthma attacks and made much less use of their inhalers than the control group. At the end of the trial, 45% of sufferers receiving Q were able to discontinue steroid treatment compared with 7% of the placebo group. The results also indicated that Q was well tolerated and that the frequency of adverse effects was low and similar to that of the control group.

a) Give THREE differences between the phase I and the phase II stages of the clinical trials described in the passage. (3)

b) What is the reason for including the control group in phase III? (2)

c) What is the evidence in the passage that drug Q is 'fit for purpose'? (2)

d) i) What is a *placebo*?
   ii) Suggest why 7% of the placebo group were able to discontinue the use of inhaled corticosteroids at the end of the phase III clinical trial. (2)

e) i) In general, would drug Q be better as an addition or an alternative to inhaled corticosteroids for sufferers of allergic asthma?
   ii) Justify your choice of answer. (2)

f) Elderly people consume more than one-third of all the drugs prescribed in the UK yet they are normally excluded from the phase I clinical trial of a new drug. Suggest TWO possible reasons for this apparent discrimination. (2)

2 Maintenance of high standards of safety is particularly important in biotechnological industries

Risk group	Level of risk to laboratory workers	Level of risk to population at large	Description of micro-organism	Level of containment required
1	low	low	It has never been identified as a pathogen and is unlikely to cause disease.	W
2	moderate	low	It can cause disease and may affect laboratory workers but is unlikely to be a serious hazard. Preventative measures and treatment are effective.	X
3	high	low	It presents a severe threat to the health of laboratory workers but not to the community in general. Preventative measures and treatment may be effective.	Y
4	high	high	It is a pathogen that causes severe illness in humans. It constitutes a potential hazard to laboratory workers and the community since it is readily transmitted from person to person. No effective treatment is available.	Z

Table 16.1

Safety precaution	Level of containment			
	W	X	Y	Z
written code of practice	+	+	+	+
manual of bio-safety	o	+	+	+
closed system in operation	o	+	+	+
presence of emergency shower facility	o	o	+	+
presence of controlled negative air pressure	o	o	o	+
presence of filters in air ducts	o	o	+	+
presence of air locks and compulsory shower for staff	o	o	o	+

Table 16.2 (+ = required, o = not required)

that make use of micro-organisms. Table 16.1 shows a classification of micro-organisms based on the level of risk and recommended level of containment. Table 16.2 gives a few examples of the safety precautions required at different levels of containment.

a) *Ebola* virus is a pathogen that destroys the inner lining of the blood vessels. It causes the victim to suffer a high fever and chronic internal bleeding. There is no known treatment and the disease is fatal in nine out of ten cases. Identify the risk level of *Ebola* to:
   i) laboratory workers
   ii) the general public.
   iii) What level of containment should be used during research work on this virus? (3)

b) The bacterium *Clostridium perfringens* is the third most common cause of food poisoning in the UK. It causes abdominal pains and diarrhoea but is fairly mild and usually resolves itself within 24 hours. Treatment is available when necessary and its spread is easily prevented by good hygienic

practices. Identify the risk level of *Clostridium perfringens* to:
   i) laboratory workers
   ii) the general public.
   iii) What level of containment should be used when working with this bacterium? (3)

c) How many levels of containment require:
   i) filters to be present in the laboratory's air ducts?
   ii) a closed system to be in operation? (2)

d) Scientists decided that a micro-organism with which they were about to work belonged to risk group 3. How many of the safety precautions listed in Table 13.2 would apply to this microbe? (1)

e) According to the information given in the tables, which safety precautions must be taken to contain a risk 4 microbe but are not required for a risk 3 microbe? (2)

Unit 3

Sustainability and Interdependence

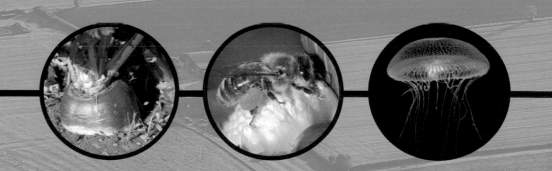

17 Food supply, plant growth and productivity

1 The graph in Figure 17.1 shows changes in per-capita agricultural production that occurred following the 'green revolution'. Draw TWO conclusions from the graph. (2)

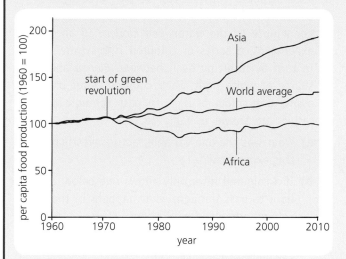

Figure 17.1

2 The Venn diagram in Figure 17.2 refers to the factors that affect food security.

a) Which number refers to people who have a constantly secure supply of food? (1)

b) Which number refers to people who live in a place where sufficient quantity and quality of food are available but they cannot afford to buy the food? (1)

c) Which number refers to people who live in a place where they can afford the food but it lacks quality and variety? (1)

d) How many areas in the diagram indicate lack of food security? (1)

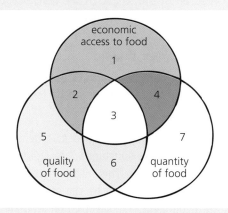

Figure 17.2

3 Figure 17.3 shows the fate of the energy present in the grass in a field when consumed by a cow.

a) Which lettered arrow represents the flow of energy from producer to consumer? (1)

b) Calculate the percentage of energy successfully converted from grass to the cow's body tissues. (1)

c) Name TWO ways in which energy could be lost by the cow at arrow X. (2)

d) Explain why the energy lost at arrow Y is not lost to the ecosystem as a whole. (1)

e) If the energy conversion efficiency of cow to human is 8%, how many of the cow's 120 kJ could have become built into human tissues? (1)

4 Imagine a sailor shipwrecked on a barren, rocky island lacking top soil. From the ship's cargo he has managed to salvage one live hen and a bag of wheat grains.

a) To make these, his only resources, last for as long as possible, which of the following courses of action should he take?

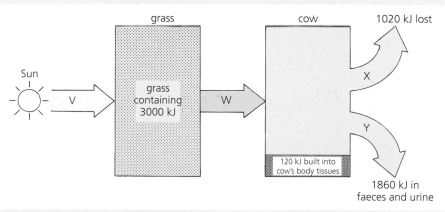

Figure 17.3

1 Eat the hen and then eat the wheat.

2 Feed all of the wheat to the hen, eat its eggs and then eat the hen when the wheat runs out.

3 Share the wheat with the hen and then eat the hen when the wheat is finished. (1)

b) Justify your choice of answer and explain why the other courses of action would be less successful. (2)

5 An Rf value is normally expressed as a decimal fraction. For example, substance X in Figure 17.4 has an Rf of 48/60 = 0.80. This means that X has moved 80% of the distance moved by the solvent. Figure 17.5 shows an incomplete thin-layer chromatogram of the four photosynthetic pigments from a green leaf.

a) Calculate the Rf of chlorophyll b. (1)

b) Copy or trace the chromatogram in Figure 17.5 and draw a spot to represent xanthophyll which has an Rf of 0.35. (1)

c) Identify pigment Y and calculate its Rf. (2)

d) Why must repeated spotting and drying of pigment extract be carried out when preparing the origin of pigment extract? (1)

e) Why must the origin be kept above the solvent level in the tube when the end of the strip is dipped into the solvent to run the chromatogram? (1)

f) Name a solvent that could be used to remove 'grass' stains from a garment at room temperature. (1)

6 Rate of photosynthesis can be measured by counting the number of oxygen bubbles released per minute by the waterweed *Elodea*. In an experiment, a series of coloured filters were used in turn by inserting each between *Elodea* and the source of white light. Each coloured filter only allows one colour of light to pass through it. The results are shown in Table 17.1.

a) What was the one variable factor investigated in this experiment? (1)

b) If a coloured filter only allows one colour of light to pass through, what happens to the other colours present in white light? (1)

c) Explain why the *mean* number of bubbles was calculated each time. (1)

d) The experiment allows a short space of time to elapse after removing one filter and before inserting the next. Suggest why? (1)

e) Present the results as a bar chart. (2)

f) Draw a conclusion from the results. (1)

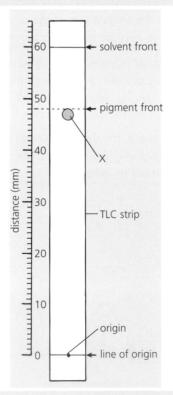

Figure 17.4

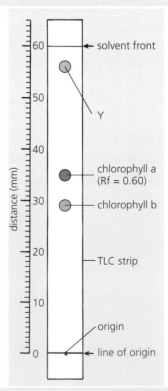

Figure 17.5

Colour of light allowed through by filter	Wavelength of light (nm)	Mean number of bubbles of oxygen released per minute
blue	430	15
green	550	1
yellow	600	4
red	640	12

Table 17.1

g) A nanometre (nm) is one-thousandth of a micrometre (μm) which is one-thousandth of a millimetre (mm) which is one-thousandth of a metre (m). Draw a table to summarise this information and include a column which expresses each unit as a fraction of a metre using negative indices. (3)

7 a) Which pair of leaf pigments combined would give the absorption spectrum shown in Figure 17.6? (2)

b) i) Which pair of pigments absorb most light energy in region Z in the graph?
ii) Is this energy used in photosynthesis?
iii) Explain your answer. (4)

8 Figure 17.7 shows the result of placing a strand of alga in a liquid containing motile aerobic bacteria and illuminating the strand with a tiny spectrum of light.

a) In which colours of light did most bacteria congregate? (2)

b) Account for this distribution of the bacteria. (2)

9 The leaves of an oak tree change from green to brown in the autumn prior to leaf fall. Outline the procedure that you would follow to investigate whether the pigment content of autumn leaves differs from that of green summer leaves. (9)

10 Redraw Figure 17.8 and construct a diagram of the light-dependent first stage of photosynthesis by completing the seven boxes using the following statements:

a) high-energy electrons transferred through electron transport chain releasing energy

b) hydrogen transferred to NADP

c) excited electrons captured by primary electron acceptor

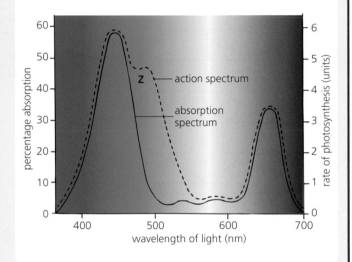

Figure 17.6

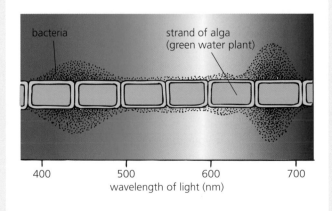

Figure 17.7

d) some energy used to generate ATP

e) light energy absorbed by chlorophyll

f) oxygen released

g) some energy used to split water. (6)

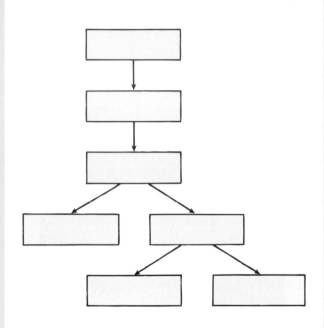

Figure 17.8

11 Figure 17.9 shows the Calvin cycle.

a) Copy the diagram and complete the blank boxes. (2)

b) i) Which chemical acts as the carbon dioxide acceptor?

ii) Add an arrow and the symbol **CO_2** to your diagram to show where CO_2 enters the cycle.

iii) Mark the letter **R** on the arrow which represents the reaction controlled by rubisco. (3)

c) i) Mark **X** on your diagram at TWO points at which ATP is needed for the cycle to turn.

ii) Why is ATP necessary at these points? (2)

d) i) Which substance would accumulate if the plant were deprived of carbon dioxide?

ii) Explain why. (2)

e) i) Which substance would accumulate if the plant were placed in darkness?

ii) Explain why. (2)

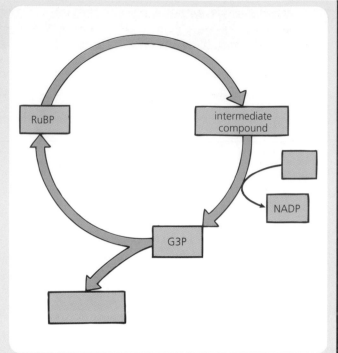

Figure 17.9

12 Figure 17.10 shows the effect of increasing light intensity on the rates of photosynthesis of a plant kept at two different concentrations of carbon dioxide.

a) What factor was limiting photosynthetic rate at region A on the graph? (1)

b) What factor was limiting photosynthetic rate at point B? (1)

c) By how many times did CO_2 concentration differ between the two experiments? (1)

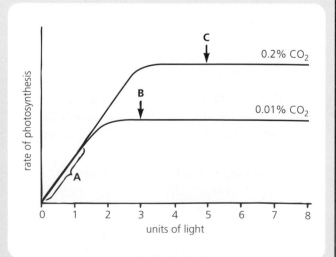

Figure 17.10

d) What experimental factor not referred to in the graph could be limiting the rate of photosynthesis at point C? (1)

13 The data in Table 17.2 refer to the results from an investigation into the effect of intercropping maize (M) with a leguminous plant (L).

Planting pattern	Density of planting (plants $10^3\,ha^{-1}$)	Dry biomass at harvest (kg)	
		Maize	Legume
1 row M:1 row L	10	4 136	2 927
	20	9 549	3 946
	30	13 817	3 233
	40	11 628	2 876
1 row M:2 rows L	10	4 385	2 112
	20	12 429	3 198
	30	14 305	2 615
	40	10 502	2 308
2 rows M:1 row L	10	5 235	2 179
	20	10 427	2 886
	30	11 493	2 513
	40	9 418	2 346
2 rows M:2 rows L	10	6 652	2 089
	20	10 418	2 517
	30	15 076	2 354
	40	11 699	1 664

Table 17.2

a) According to these results what is the optimum density of planting for:
 i) maize?
 ii) legume? (2)

b) According to these results which planting pattern is most productive for:
 i) maize?
 ii) legume? (2)

c) What controls should have been run in this experiment? (1)

d) How could the reliability of the results be improved? (1)

14 A crop plant's productivity was investigated on a warm, sunny day by cutting leaf discs from the plant at hourly intervals and drying these to constant mass. The results are shown in Table 17.3.

Time on 24-hour clock	Biomass of discs (g)
06.00	4.02
07.00	4.04
08.00	4.08
09.00	4.16
10.00	4.27
11.00	4.40
12.00	4.52
13.00	4.63
14.00	4.72
15.00	4.80
16.00	4.87
17.00	4.89
18.00	5.00
19.00	5.02
20.00	5.02
21.00	5.00
22.00	4.96

Table 17.3

a) Present the data as a line graph (with the points joined up using a ruler). (3)

b) Between which two times was the rate of productivity greatest? (1)

c) Calculate the mean gain in biomass of the discs per hour for:
 i) the period between 10.00 and 13.00
 ii) the period between 13.00 and 16.00. (2)

d) Suggest why rate of productivity was greater during the morning than during the afternoon. (1)

e) Account for the trend shown after 20.00 hours. (1)

f) Give an example of a piece of scientific procedure that should be carried out in this experiment to avoid introducing further variable factors. (1)

g) i) Which result appears to be an outlier?
 ii) Suggest how this might have arisen. (2)

15 The information in Table 17.4 refers to the average values for a farm's maize crop.

Part of maize plant	Dry mass per plant (g)
roots	44
leaves	140
stem	200
grain	216

Table 17.4

a) Calculate this farm's harvest index for maize as a percentage. (1)

b) Why is harvest index always less than 100%? (1)

16 Give an account of the trapping and transfer of energy that occurs during photosynthesis from light energy present in the Sun's rays to chemical energy contained in sugar. (9)

18 Plant and animal breeding

1 In pea plants the gene for pod type has two alleles, inflated and constricted, as shown in Figure 18.1.

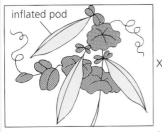
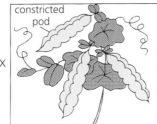

parents (both true-breeding)

inflated pod X constricted pod

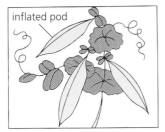

F₁ generation inflated pod

Figure 18.1

a) Which allele is dominant? Explain your answer. (2)

b) Using letters of your choice, give the genotype of the F₁ generation. (1)

c) A further generation of pea plants was produced by allowing the F₁ generation to self-pollinate. Using your chosen symbols, copy and complete Table 16.1 to show the outcome of this cross. (4)

		Genotypes of pollen	
Genotypes of ovules			

Table 18.1

d) The F₂ generation consists of 1180 plants. In theory how many would be
  i) homozygous for inflated pod?
  ii) heterozygous for inflated pod?
  iii) constricted pod? (3)

e) i) Is pod type an example of *discrete* or *continuous* variation?
  ii) Justify your answer to **i)**. (2)

2 In tomato plants, fruit colour may be red or yellow. Table 18.2 gives details of crosses between certain tomato plants and the offspring produced in each case.

a) Using letters of your choice, identify the genotypes of tomato plants A, B, C, D, E and F. (6)

b) Which cross could have been a test cross to check if one of the plants was homozygous or heterozygous? (1)

3 Weaning weight is the weight of a calf when it changes its food from milk to solids. It is a polygenic characteristic in cattle. The sum of all the additive effects of the genes controlling a polygenic trait is called the breeding value for that trait. Table 18.3 shows the effects of the alleles of four genes on weaning weight in a breed of cattle. Table 18.4 shows the breeding values of weaning weight for five animals.

Supply the information missing from boxes **a)**, **b)** and **c)** in Table 18.4. (3)

4 Figure 18.2 shows a field trial of plots set up to investigate the effect of nitrogenous fertiliser and fungicide on a new cultivar of cereal crop. Figure 18.3 (see page 67) shows the results at the end of the growing season as total dry mass (kg) per plot.

a) How many variable factors were investigated in this crop field trial? (1)

Cross	Parents	Number and phenotype(s) of offspring
1	plant A (red) × plant B (red)	258 red
2	plant B (red) × plant C (red)	197 red and 65 yellow
3	plant D (red) × plant E (yellow)	128 red and 134 yellow
4	plant E (yellow) × plant F (yellow)	261 yellow

Table 18.2

Gene controlling weaning weight	Alleles of gene	Effect on weaning weight (kg)
1	W^1	+6
	w^1	0
2	W^2	+8
	w^2	0
3	W^3	+3
	w^3	0
4	W^4	+10
	w^4	0

Table 18.3

Animal	Genotype Alleles of gene								Breeding value (for weaning weight)
	1		2		3		4		
P	W^1	W^1	W^2	W^2	W^3	W^3	W^4	W^4	6+6+8+8+3+3+10+10 = 54 kg
Q	W^1	w^1	w^2	w^2	W^3	w^3	W^4	W^4	6+0+0+0+3+0+10+10 = 29 kg
R	w^1	w^1	W^2	w^2	w^3	w^3	W^4	w^4	a)
S	W^1	W^1	w^2	w^2	W^3	w^3	W^4	W^4	b)
T	c)								6+0+8+0+3+0+10+0 = 27 kg

Table 18.4

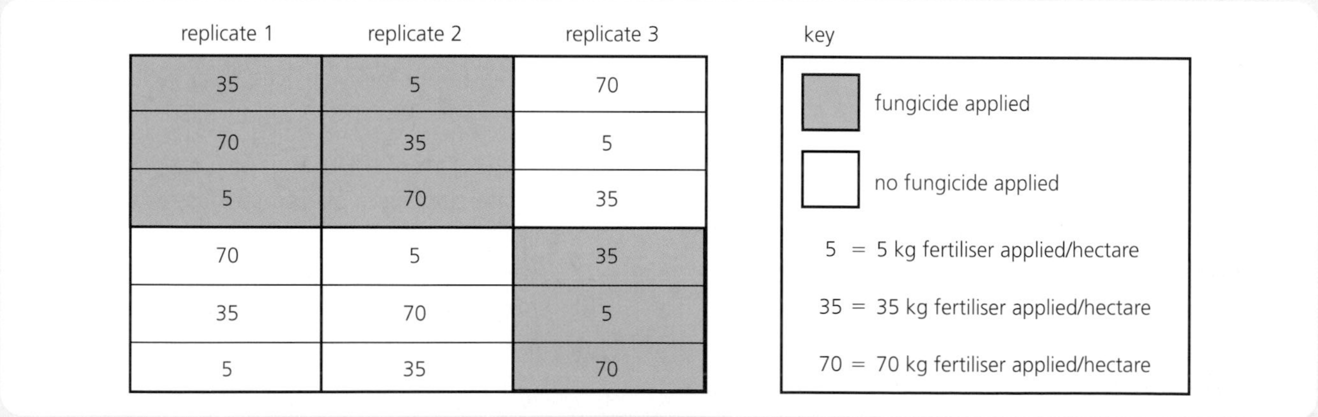

replicate 1	replicate 2	replicate 3
35	5	70
70	35	5
5	70	35
70	5	35
35	70	5
5	35	70

key

fungicide applied

no fungicide applied

5 = 5 kg fertiliser applied/hectare

35 = 35 kg fertiliser applied/hectare

70 = 70 kg fertiliser applied/hectare

Figure 18.2

b) How many treatments of
   i) fertiliser were used?
   ii) fungicide were used? (2)

c) State ONE design feature that helped to ensure that a fair comparison of treatments could be made. (1)

d) Identify ONE design feature that took into account variability among samples and reduced the effect of experimental error. (1)

e) What was done to eliminate the chance of the results being biased? (1)

f) **i)** Table 18.5 has been drawn up to record and view the results (as kg total dry mass per plot) in an organised way. The values of replicate 1's

Fungicide or no fungicide	Fertiliser treatment (kg/acre)	Replicate 1	Replicate 2	Replicate 3
no fungicide	5	201		
	35	304		
	70	316		
fungicide	5	252		
	35	371		
	70	379		

Table 18.5

replicate 1	replicate 2	replicate 3
371	258	329
379	366	207
252	383	305
316	211	364
304	327	249
201	312	386

Figure 18.3

plots have been entered. Copy and complete the table.

ii) From your completed version of Table 16.5 draw a conclusion about the effect of the fungicide on this new cultivar of cereal crop and explain your answer.

iii) Why would it be necessary to apply statistical analysis to the results before being able to draw a conclusion about the effect of the two higher concentrations of fertiliser on the crop? (6)

g) What control should have been run in this field trial? (1)

5 A breed of pig has been produced which reaches bacon weight in 150 days instead of the normal 185 days. In addition, this is achieved on 20% less food. Can this improvement process be continued indefinitely? Explain your answer. (2)

6 The graph in Figure 18.4 shows the effect of continuous inbreeding on heterozygosity.

a) Starting with a genotype heterozygous for 15 genes, what percentage of heterozygosity remains in the F_5 generation? (1)

b) Starting with a genotype heterozygous for 10 genes, what decrease in heterozygosity has occurred by the F_3 generation? (1)

c) Which genotype's heterozygosity has decreased by 75% at the F_2 generation? (1)

d) At which generation was the heterozygosity of all four genotypes first found to be below 10%? (1)

7 Read the passage and answer the questions that follow it.

New cultivar of maize

Native Americans began growing maize (which originated in Mexico) as a food crop thousands of years ago. This resulted in the development of many strains adapted to a wide range of conditions from tropical to cool, temperate climates. Maize brought to Europe hundreds of years ago was developed by breeding and selection as a Mediterranean crop suited to the warm, dry conditions of Southern Europe. These cultivars were found to be unsuited to conditions such as those that occur in Northern Scotland.

However, production of maize in northern regions is now increasing substantially following the development in France of cultivars developed specially for use in cold, temperate areas. These new varieties are the result of complicated breeding programmes involving crosses between European and North American strains.

The cultivars succeed in the north of Scotland because they contain alleles of genes that:

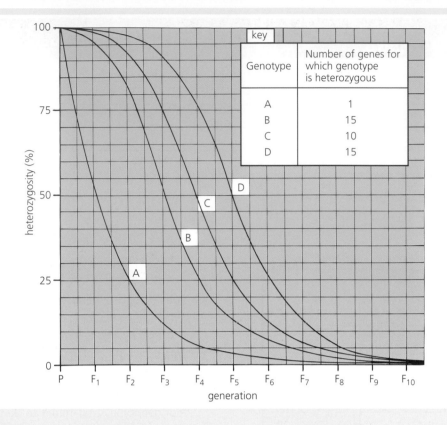

Figure 18.4

- allow them to mature early thereby enabling them to make the most of the shorter growing season in the north
- make them suitable for use on marginal sites
- enable them to be easily fertilised
- make them produce good, solid cobs with a high starch content that make excellent feed for ruminant animals.

a) Why were the earlier cultivars, bred directly from maize brought to Europe from America hundreds of years ago, unsuited to conditions in Northern Scotland? (2)

b) By what means has the new cultivar, suited to northern areas, been developed? (2)

c) In what way is this new cultivar able to cope with the shorter growing season in the north of Scotland? (1)

d) **i)** Name TWO ruminants commonly found in Scottish farms.
ii) Why is the new cultivar of maize favoured by farmers of ruminant animals? (3)

e) Figure 18.5 shows one maize plant from cultivar A and one maize plant from cultivar B.
i) Briefly outline the procedure that you would

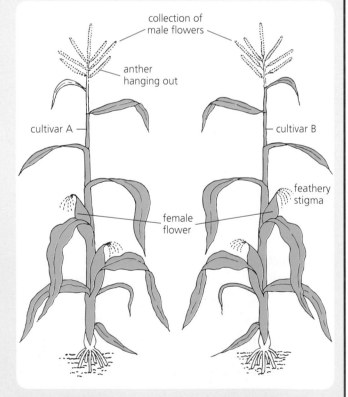

Figure 18.5

	Genotype	Weight gained by phenotype per day (kg)
parent 1	AAbb	0.82
parent 2	aaBB	0.82
F₁ generation	AaBb	1.00

Table 18.6

adopt if you wanted to inbreed each cultivar and prevent it from outbreeding.

ii) Briefly outline the procedure you would adopt to crossbreed the two cultivars and prevent them from inbreeding. (4)

8 Table 18.6 refers to a breeding experiment involving cattle. What can be concluded from the data? (2)

9 When a tomato fruit is fully grown, but still green and unripe, it begins to produce ethylene. Ethylene is a growth substance which promotes the ripening of fruit. Genetic engineers have developed a variety of tomato plant which makes very little ethylene by inserting a gene which almost completely blocks ethylene production. Table 18.7 gives the results from one of their experiments. Figure 18.6 shows a typical fruit from each variety of tomato plant.

a) Draw a line graph of the results. (2)

b) Match the terms *control* and *genetically modified variety* with the two lettered varieties in the diagram. (1)

c) State how many units of ethylene were produced on day 6 by:
i) the genetically modified variety
ii) the control. (1)

d) Calculate the percentage decrease in ethylene production at day 6 caused by the blocked gene in the genetically modified variety. (1)

e) Suggest why it is important that ethylene production is not completely blocked in the modified variety. (1)

f) What is the benefit gained from this application of genetic engineering? (1)

10 Give an account of selective breeding and hybridisation of food crops and domesticated animals. (9)

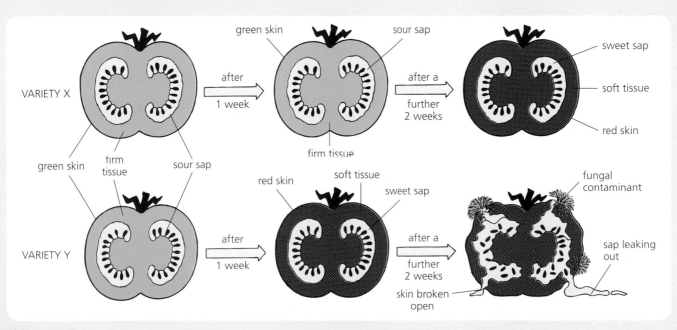

Figure 18.6

Time from green fruit reaching full size (days)	Ethylene production (units)	
	Genetically modified variety	Control
0	1	1
1	4	5
2	7	25
3	5	70
4	6	71
5	8	68
6	7	70
7	6	52
8	7	41
9	7	32
10	8	34
11	6	31
12	7	32
13	7	29
14	8	32
15	7	31
16	6	28
17	8	25
18	7	26
19	7	23
20	6	21
21	6	19

Table 18.7

19 Crop protection

1 The seven pairs of characteristics listed below refer to a certain **weed species** and to a related **non-weed species**. Construct a table with these two emboldened terms as its headings. Consider each pair of characteristics and then enter each member of the pair in the appropriate column in the table. (Keep in mind that a weed needs to be an opportunist to survive.) (7)

- can grow well on poor soil/needs fertile soil to grow well
- requires short days to flower/able to flower in any day length
- quick to flower and produce many tiny seeds/slow to flower and produce a few large seeds
- self-pollinated/cross-pollinated
- intolerant of drought/tolerant of drought
- tolerant of water-logged soil/intolerant of water-logged soil
- long life cycle/short life cycle

2 'Seed' potatoes are grown and retained to generate future crops. 'Ware' potatoes are grown for consumption and are not retained for further use. Ware potatoes may be grown anywhere but seed potatoes may only be grown on land that has been tested for potato cyst nematodes (PCN) and has been given a clearance certificate. The chart in Figure 19.1 outlines the test in a simple way.

a) Match the following four test outcomes with boxes P, Q, R and S in the chart. (3)
   i) Soil may be used for ware potatoes and varieties of seed potato resistant to PCN.
   ii) Soil may not be used for seed potatoes and its use for commercial growth of ware potatoes is not advised.
   iii) Soil may be used for ware potatoes *and* seed potatoes.
   iv) Soil may not be used for seed potatoes but may be used for ware potatoes.

b) Damage to potato crops by PCN is patchy. It tends to be most severe where the soil is very wet or very dry and the growing conditions for the potato plants are stressful. Suggest how PCN damage could be reduced in these areas without using protective chemicals. (2)

c) Hatching of viable cysts can be triggered by a chemical given out by the roots of potato

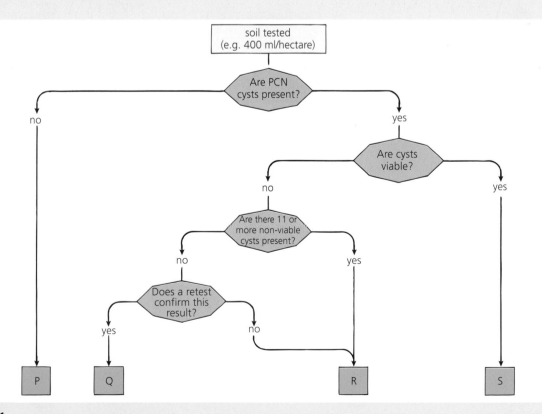

Figure 19.1

plants in spring. If scientists could find a way of synthesising this chemical, suggest how it might be used to control PCN. (2)

d) **i)** Which would be a more effective means of controlling PCN: a crop rotation of 4 years or of 7 years?

   ii) Explain your answer. (2)

3 Figure 19.2 shows the life cycle of a fungal pathogen called smut that affects cereal plants such as wheat.

a) Identify by its number, the stage that supports each of the following statements:

   i) the parasite can survive without the host over winter

   ii) the host plant's metabolism suffers

   iii) the host plant fails to make seed grains

   iv) germination conditions that suit seed grains also suit the pathogen

   v) the parasite has an enormous reproductive capacity. (5)

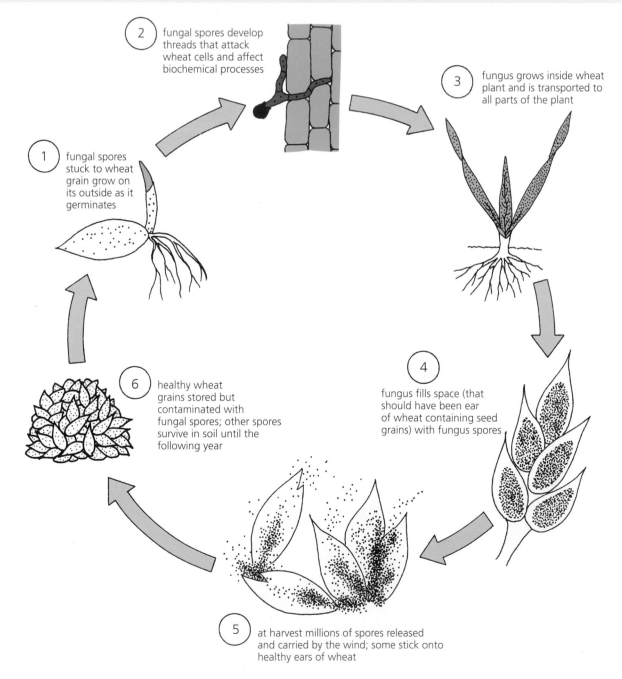

2 fungal spores develop threads that attack wheat cells and affect biochemical processes

3 fungus grows inside wheat plant and is transported to all parts of the plant

1 fungal spores stuck to wheat grain grow on its outside as it germinates

4 fungus fills space (that should have been ear of wheat containing seed grains) with fungus spores

6 healthy wheat grains stored but contaminated with fungal spores; other spores survive in soil until the following year

5 at harvest millions of spores released and carried by the wind; some stick onto healthy ears of wheat

Figure 19.2

Field number	Time during growing season when field was weeded	Yield of cereal grain (kg ha^{-1})		
		Mass of nitrogenous fertiliser added (kg ha^{-1})		
		0.0	0.5	5.0
1	all season	2576	2981	3400
2	early season only	2243	2349	3032
3	mid-season only	2065	2197	2842
4	late season only	1472	1774	2087

Table 19.1

b) i) At which numbered stage in this pathogen's life cycle would it be best to apply a fungicide?
ii) Explain your answer. (2)

4 An investigation was carried out on the effect of concentration of nitrogenous fertiliser and time of weeding on the grain yield of a cereal crop. Table 19.1 shows the results.

a) i) What was the effect of added nitrogen on yield of cereal grain?
ii) Account for this effect. (2)

b) i) What was the effect of time of weeding on yield of grain?
ii) If the farmer could only afford to weed the field once, when would be the best time to do it?
iii) Explain your choice of answer to ii) with reference to competition. (4)

c) Calculate the percentage increase in yield that the addition of 5 kg ha^{-1} of fertiliser brought about for field 1 compared with the addition of no fertiliser. (1)

d) Suggest TWO factors in addition to nitrogen that the crop plants and the weeds may be competing for. (2)

e) 1 hectare (ha) = 10 000 m^2. Convert 3400 kg ha^{-1} into g m^{-2}. (1)

5 Figure 19.3 shows ten conversation bubbles.

a) i) Make a list of the letters that represent the five people who are stating an opinion that is against the use of pesticides.
ii) Pair each letter in your list with one of the remaining statements where a person presents a counter argument in favour of pesticide use. (4)

b) i) Are you for or against the use of pesticides on food crops?
ii) Give ONE reason why you take this position.

6 Figure 19.4 (see page 77) shows a graph of the results from an investigation into the effect of two fungicides on potato plants.

a) How many days did it take for the untreated potato plants to show a level of 75% infection? (1)

b) By how many did the number of infected plants treated with contact fungicide exceed the number of infected plants treated with systemic fungicide 33 days after spraying? (1)

c) By how many times was the number of untreated infected plants at day 21 greater than the number of infected plants treated with systemic fungicide? (1)

d) Among plants treated with contact fungicide, what percentage increase in number of infected plants occurred between day 21 and day 35? (1)

e) i) Which type of fungicide is more effective?
ii) Explain your choice of answer. (2)

7 A wide variety of fungi attack crop plants. A few are listed in Table 19.2.

Such fungal attack can often be prevented by spraying the surface of the potential host plant with fungicide. This reduces the number of fungal spores which germinate. A chemical company set out to investigate the effectiveness of two new fungicides (A and B). Petri dishes of nutrient agar containing fungicide were inoculated with fungal spores. Table 19.3 (see page 77) shows the results. Table 19.4 (see page 78) gives further information about the two fungicides.

a) Give the scientific names of TWO fungal pathogens to which wheat can play host. (1)

b) Why was each condition of the experiment set up in *triplicate*? (1)

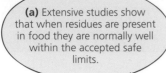

(a) Extensive studies show that when residues are present in food they are normally well within the accepted safe limits.

(b) Neighbouring land is often polluted with pesticides when farmers spray their crops.

(c) Regular health checks on people who work with pesticides daily and wear protective clothing show no ill effects.

(d) Most food is treated with pesticide during its production and/or storage, therefore people are taking in harmful pesticides in their food.

(e) Most of the pesticides approved for use in the UK leave no detectable residue in the environment and those that do are controlled by regulations.

(f) Control of pests by cultural means is rarely sufficiently effective on its own and chemical back-up is often needed.

(g) All pesticides work against living organisms and leave harmful residues behind in the environment.

(h) Farm workers are adversely affected when applying chemicals to crops on a regular basis.

(i) Farmers are obliged to use chemicals according to careful instructions and breaking these rules is punishable by a fine.

(j) Chemical protection of crops should be replaced completely by cultural means of control.

Figure 19.3

c) Summarise, in turn, the effect of fungicides A and B on fungus Z. (1)

d) Summarise, in turn, the effect of fungicides A and B on fungus Y. (1)

e) Which fungicide had the greater overall effect on:
i) fungus W?
ii) fungus X?
iii) Which concentration of which fungicide prevented all of fungus W's spores from germinating? (2)

f) i) State the average percentage germination of spores from fungus X under control conditions.

ii) Calculate the reduction in percentage germination of spores caused by applying 5 ppm of fungicide B to fungus X. (2)

g) Experts claim that fungicides A and B tend to show a degree of specificity in their action. Justify this claim with reference to the data. (1)

h) The chemical company running the trials found that they could only afford to continue with one of the fungicides. Suggest TWO reasons why they chose A in preference to B. (2)

Scientific name	Symbol for easy reference	Disease caused	Host plant affected
Erysiphe graminis	W	mildew	wheat and barley
Urcinula necator	X	mildew	grapevine
Puccinia graminis	Y	black rust	wheat
Phytophthora infestans	Z	blight	potato

Table 19.2

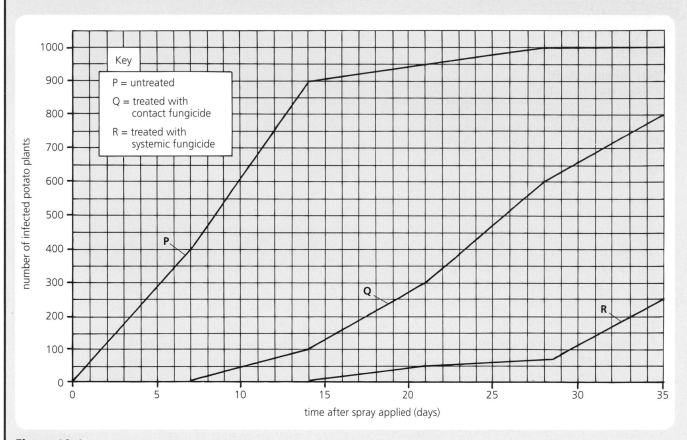

Figure 19.4

	Concentration of fungicide (ppm)	Plate	% germination of fungal spores			
			Fungus W	Fungus X	Fungus Y	Fungus Z
Control	0	1	100	97	77	44
		2	99	100	74	41
		3	100	100	76	43
Fungicide A	5	1	20	5	76	45
		2	23	9	75	41
		3	22	7	76	43
	50	1	0	0	49	44
		2	0	0	48	42
		3	0	0	49	43
Fungicide B	5	1	100	60	76	43
		2	97	62	76	42
		3	100	61	77	44
	50	1	18	5	76	42
		2	17	7	78	43
		3	19	6	74	44

Table 19.3

	Fungicide A		Fungicide B	
Concentration (ppm)	5	50	5	50
Toxic effect on wildlife	none	very slight	very slight	slight
Effect on host plant (% reduction in yield)	0	3	0	1
Projected cost of spray	cheap	fairly cheap	very cheap	cheap
Biodegradable?	yes		yes	

Table 19.4

8 Many years ago, farmers in Peru began using vast quantities of pesticide containing DDT on their crops to control insects. They enjoyed record harvests for three successive years and then the problems began. Their crops suffered infestations of aphids and boll weevils which were unaffected by DDT treatment. Within 5 years the farmers were worse off than they were at the start.

　a) Why were the aphids and boll weevils unaffected by DDT treatment after 5 years? (1)

　b) Account for the increase in population numbers of the pests using the following terms in your answer: *natural selection, resistant strain, selection pressure, pesticide, competition*. (5)

9 Dieldrin is a type of pesticide which was used in Britain in the 1950s to dress wheat grain against attack by insects. During each year of its use,

thousands of seed-eating birds were found to be poisoned. In the 1960s a severe decline in number of peregrine falcons occurred (see Figure 19.5) and many of the survivors were found to have high concentrations of dieldrin in their bodies. The females produced eggs with thinner shells.

　a) Construct a food chain to include the organisms named above. (1)

　b) Low concentrations of dieldrin were used to dress the grain, yet high concentrations were found in the falcons' bodies. Explain fully how this difference arose. (2)

　c) During which of the following intervals of time did the number of breeding pairs decrease at the fastest rate? (1)

　　A 1956–58　B 1958–60　C 1960–62　D 1962–64

　d) Calculate the percentage decrease in breeding pairs that occurred between 1957 and 1964. (1)

　e) Why does production of thinner egg shells lead to a reduction in number of future breeding pairs? (1)

　f) Account for the trend shown in the graph from 1965 onwards. (1)

10 Give an account of crop protection under the following headings:

　a) control by cultural means (3)

　b) chemical control (4)

　c) biological control. (2)

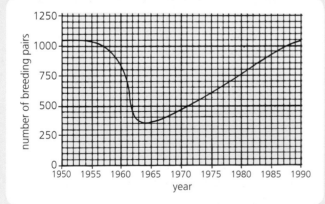

Figure 19.5

20 Animal welfare

1 In the UK a small percentage of dairy cattle are housed all year round with little or no access to grazing. This makes the management of the cows easier for the farmer but it begs the question: *'Do these cows enjoy a satisfactory standard of welfare?'*

Here are some comments made about this practice:

1) The cows are protected from adverse weather.

2) Insufficient space is available for the cows to move around freely.

3) The risk of injury and lameness is increased by hard, concrete flooring.

4) There is a lower risk of exposure to airborne diseases and TB from badgers.

5) The composition of feed can be carefully controlled to suit the cows' requirements.

6) The cows are denied the opportunity to walk on soft, non-slip pasture.

7) The risk of infestation by parasites is greatly reduced.

8) The cows cannot pursue their natural urge to forage.

a) Classify statements 1)–8) into:
  i) those in support of and
  ii) those against the practice of all-year-round housing for dairy cattle. (2)

b) i) In your opinion, which TWO of the five freedoms for animal welfare are cows that are housed all year round being denied?
  ii) Justify your choice of answer. (2)

c) Suggest a compromise that might be acceptable to both sides in this argument. (1)

2 Table 20.1 refers to the results of a survey carried out on risk factors associated with three types of henhouse.

a) i) Risk factors 3 and 5 show the same pattern of risk level. Suggest why.
  ii) Which other TWO risk factors show the same pattern? (2)

b) Which risk factor appears to be unaffected by the type of accommodation that the chickens receive? (1)

c) i) Which type of accommodation runs a high risk of the birds being affected by internal parasites?
  ii) Suggest why this should be the case? (2)

d) i) Which birds are least likely to suffer low bone strength?
  ii) Suggest why. (2)

e) i) What effect does leaving beaks untrimmed have on feather-pecking in caged birds?
  ii) Explain why. (2)

f) i) Using the system high risk = 2 points, medium risk = 1 point, low risk = 0 points, work out the overall level of risk for each type of accommodation.
  ii) Suggest how risk of bumble foot disease could be reduced.
  iii) If bumble foot were eradicated completely, in what way would this shift the balance of overall level of risk for the three types of accommodation? (4)

3 Read the passage and answer the questions that follow it.

'Chemical welfare'

Many diseases caused by bacteria, viruses and protozoa (single-celled animals) are carried by insect vectors and affect livestock. Where intensive farming methods are practised, it is not unusual for several thousand poultry or pigs to be reared on a farm at the same time. This situation creates the perfect conditions for an epidemic to occur. Therefore, in addition to maintaining high standards of hygiene, farmers often make use of chemicals to prevent an outbreak of disease. These treatments include pesticides, vaccines and, in some countries, antibiotics in the animal feed.

Free-grazing animals such as sheep and cattle are also vulnerable to various ailments. Some of these are caused by pests such as scab mites and ticks that pierce the animal's skin. These external parasites can be controlled by dipping the farm animal in pesticide which works by paralysing the pest's nervous system.

However some parasites live inside the host. Liver flukes, for example, spend one part of their life cycle in the mammalian host and another part in a type of snail that thrives in water-logged pasture. This problem can be tackled by using drugs to kill the parasite within the sheep or cow and/or draining the pasture and spraying it with molluscicide.

Risk factor that could affect animal's welfare	Level of risk		
	Type of accommodation		
	A conventional cage with minimal facilities in henhouse	B furnished cage with nesting boxes and perches in henhouse	C uncaged nesting boxes and perches in henhouse with free access to outside area
1 feather-pecking in beak-trimmed flock	low risk	low risk	low risk
2 feather-pecking in non-beak-trimmed flock	high risk	high risk	medium risk
3 restriction of wing-flapping movements	high risk	high risk	low risk
4 prevention of foraging	high risk	medium risk	low risk
5 restriction of tail-wagging movements	high risk	high risk	medium risk
6 bumble foot disease caused by poorly-designed perches	low risk	medium risk	high risk
7 low bone strength	high risk	medium risk	low risk
8 predation	low risk	low risk	medium risk
9 internal parasites	low risk	low risk	high risk
10 external parasites	medium risk	low risk	low risk

Key:

low risk	
medium risk	
high risk	

Table 20.1

a) To which of the five freedoms for animal welfare do the chemicals mentioned in the passage make a contribution? (1)

b) i) Why are antibiotics added to the animal feed in some countries, when the animals are perfectly healthy?
   ii) If some bacteria for a disease just happened to be resistant to the antibiotic, what problem could arise? (3)

c) i) Identify a precaution that must be taken by the workforce operating a sheep dip.
   ii) Explain your answer to i). (2)

d) The concentration of active ingredient in a brand of sheep dip chemical is 250 mg l^{-1}. Express this as
   i) g l^{-1}
   ii) µg l^{-1}. (2)

e) i) With reference to the control of liver flukes, which treatment is *preventative* and which is *curative*?
   ii) Why is prevention better than cure? (3)

4 Table 20.2 shows the various types of behaviour exhibited by a 20-day-old chicken observed over a period of time divided into 10-second intervals. A small quantity of food mixed with straw was present on the cage floor at the start. The only source of drinking water was present in a shallow dish.

a) What name is given to a list of observed behaviours? (1)

b) How long was the complete period of observation? (1)

c) Calculate the percentage time spent on each activity and present the data as a bar chart. (4)

Time interval	Category of behaviour that dominated the time interval				
	Pecking the floor	Feeding	Drinking	Preening feathers	Resting
1	*				
2	*				
3		*			
4		*			
5			*		
6					*
7				*	
8				*	
9	*				
10	*				
11	*				
12		*			
13		*			
14				*	
15					*
16				*	
17	*				
18	*				
19		*			
20		*			

Table 20.2

d) **i)** During which time intervals was the chicken's behaviour most likely to have been driven by the need to find food?
ii) What name is given to such driven behaviour? (2)

e) One hypothesis based on the results is 'The chicken only pecks the cage floor if food is present on the floor'.
i) How could this hypothesis be put to the test?
ii) What results would need to be obtained to show that the hypothesis was supported? (2)

f) If the hypothesis were supported, what would need to be done to increase the reliability of the results? (1)

5 Read the passage and answer the questions that follow it.

Birds such as fowl are often housed in conditions of excessively high stocking density and bright lighting even when they are known to prefer dim light. In these crowded conditions the birds lack the opportunity to forage. This is because they are denied access to flooring material such as straw that would enable them to peck in a natural way. In addition they have no access to alternative pecking substrates such as bunches of string and pecking blocks.

Birds in an environment lacking basic facilities may express their discomfort in several ways. One of these is inappropriate pecking behaviour which may take the form of pecking at or plucking out their own feathers or those of nearby birds.

Fowl are strongly attracted to damaged feathers and the presence of a few among a flock can be enough to set off a chain reaction of injurious pecking and cannibalism. This rarely happens if the strain of bird has been selectively bred for a reduced level of inappropriate pecking. If the inappropriate pecking continues then chicken farmers using intensive methods and very basic standards of housing for their chickens may have to resort to the use of anti-pecking sprays if things get out of hand.

a) Why do some chickens peck one another in an inappropriate way? (1)

b) Copy and complete Figure 20.1 to show FIVE ways in which attempts could be made to reduce inappropriate pecking behaviour. (Base your answers on information in the text.) (5)

c) i) Which of your answers to b) is a short-term method suitable for use only in a crisis?
   ii) Identify such a crisis from the passage. (2)

6 Give an account of the ways in which the behaviour of domesticated animals indicates that their level of welfare is poor. (9)

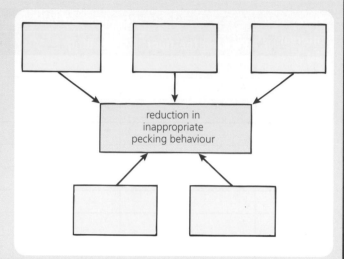

Figure 20.1

21 Symbiosis

1 Classify the following examples of symbiosis into TWO named categories:

a) Certain bacteria in the human colon feed on unwanted food, releasing vitamin B absorbed by humans.

b) Female mosquitoes suck human blood to nourish their eggs.

c) The life cycle of the Chinese liver fluke involves three different hosts (man, snail and fish).

d) Egyptian plover birds clean leeches from between the teeth of crocodiles.

e) Dodder is a flowering plant which grows attached to stinging nettle plants from which it obtains all of its food.

f) Certain fungi on the roots of pine trees aid water absorption by the tree and receive carbohydrate from it.

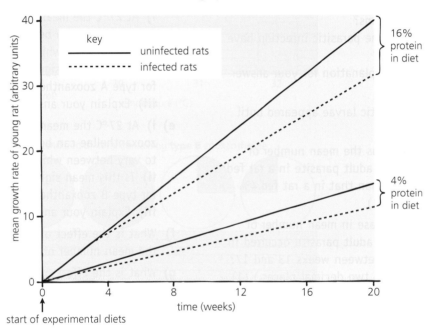

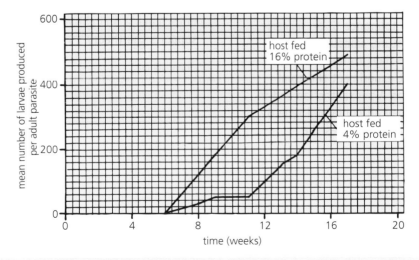

Figure 21.1

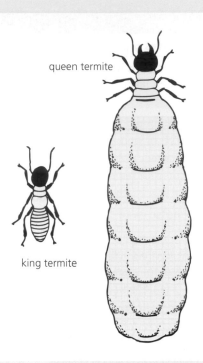

queen termite

king termite

Figure 22.2

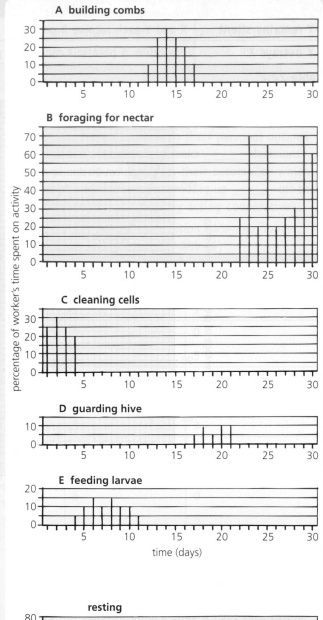

A building combs

B foraging for nectar

percentage of worker's time spent on activity

C cleaning cells

D guarding hive

E feeding larvae

time (days)

composed of males and females. The soldiers guard the nest against attacks by ants. The workers, with the aid of cellulose-digesting micro-organisms, break down wood and decaying vegetation into food.

By looking after the nest and the royal couple so effectively, the sterile lower castes ensure that the genes they have in common with their close relatives that are able to reproduce, are passed on to the next generation.

a) Identify TWO differences and TWO similarities between a society of termites and one of honeybees. (4)

b) i) Briefly describe a symbiotic relationship that involves termites.
ii) Which of the two types of symbiosis does this exemplify? (3)

5 The stick graph in Figure 22.3 shows a record of five of the tasks (A–E) performed by a worker bee during the first 30 days of her adult life and the time she spent resting.

a) Put the five tasks into the sequence in which she carried them out during these 30 days. (1)

b) Identify the days when she was employed on two tasks and name the tasks. (2)

c) Calculate the total number of hours that she spent cleaning cells in the hive. (1)

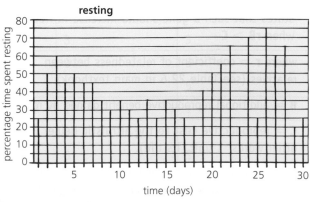

resting

percentage time spent resting

time (days)

Figure 22.3

Age and gender of ape	Mean number of times box was chosen	
	Banana	Dead spider
mature males	7.9 (+)	2.1 (−)
juvenile males	5.2	4.8
mature females	7.4 (+)	2.6 (−)
juvenile females	5.3	4.7

(+/− = value significantly higher/lower than expected by chance alone)

Table 22.3

d) During the days that she built combs, what was her percentage mean time per day devoted to this task? (1)

e) i) Compare days 23 and 24 with reference to percentage time spent foraging and resting.
ii) Give a possible explanation for the differences you gave as your answer to i). (4)

6 Read the passage and answer the questions that follow it.

A typical group of gorillas consists of one mature, silver-back male, three adult females and several youngsters. Normally the adults have all originated from different social groups because male and female gorillas, on reaching puberty, emigrate from their troop of birth.

The first female to be made part of his group by a lone silver-back male holds the highest rank. The last female to join the group holds the lowest rank. The highest-ranking female and her offspring are allowed to remain closest to the silver-back male. When a silver-back is old and ready to die, one of his sons may inherit the group on reaching sexual maturity.

a) i) Describe the social hierarchy that exists among the females in a group of gorillas.
ii) Which gorilla is least likely to benefit from this arrangement when the group is under attack?
iii) Suggest why the silver-back does not offer equal protection to all the females and their offspring in such a crisis. (3)

b) i) By what means is inbreeding among the members of a social group of gorillas prevented?

ii) When might this mechanism break down and allow inbreeding to occur? (2)

7 In an investigation into the ability of apes to read emotional expressions on a human face, a scientist sat on one side of a transparent screen with two boxes on the table in front of her. On the other side of the screen sat an ape, unable to see inside the boxes. The scientist looked inside one box which, unknown to the ape, contained a piece of banana and smiled with pleasure. Next she looked inside the other box which, unknown to the ape, contained a dead spider and expressed disgust. The ape was then allowed to reach through a hole in the screen and choose a box. The procedure was repeated ten times for each ape and many apes were used. The results are shown in Table 22.3.

a) i) What conclusion can be drawn about the effect of age on the ability of apes to read emotions on a human face?
ii) Explain your answer to i) with reference to the data.
iii) Construct an hypothesis to account for the conclusion you arrived at in i). (3)

b) i) What conclusion may be drawn about the effect of gender on the ability of apes to read emotions on a human face?
ii) Explain your answer to i). (2)

c) In repeats of the procedure, why did the scientist vary the positions of the two boxes and the order in which she looked into them before expressing an emotion. (2)

8 Give an account of ritualistic display and appeasement behaviours as exhibited by social primates. (9)

23 Mass extinction and biodiversity

1 Figure 23.1 shows five of Britain's extinct mammals.

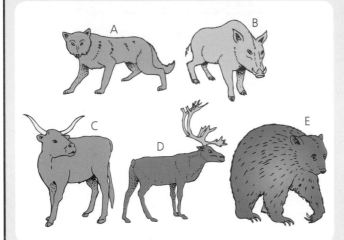

Figure 23.1

a) Match these animals with the following descriptions:

i) Ancestor of modern cattle. Became extinct in Britain in the eleventh century due to habitat destruction and over-hunting.

ii) Herbivorous mammal hunted to extinction in Britain in the tenth century. Continues to survive in some parts of Europe.

iii) Ancestor of modern pig. Hunted to extinction in Britain in the seventeenth century.

iv) Large omnivorous mammal. Became extinct in Britain during the tenth century due to habitat destruction and over-hunting.

v) Ancestor of modern dog. Hunted to extinction in Britain in the eighteenth century. (1)

b) Which of these mammals was successfully reintroduced to Scotland in 1952 and now survives as herds in the Cairngorms? (1)

c) Which of these mammals is extinct worldwide? (1)

d) Which of these mammals might possess alleles for disease resistance which could be introduced into a domesticated variety of farm animal? (1)

Geological era	Geological period	Millions of years from present	Major developments as indicated by fossil record
Cenozoic	Quaternary	present to 1	herbaceous angiosperms continue to increase; forests in decline; some tree species threatened with extinction
	Tertiary	1 to 65	angiosperms dominate; herbaceous plants increase; forests extend worldwide and then go into decline
Mesozoic	Cretaceous	65 to 140	advanced conifers decline; angiosperms dominate, some as trees
	Jurassic	140 to 205	advanced conifers dominate; primitive conifers disappear; earliest angiosperms (flowering plants) appear
	Triassic	205 to 245	seed ferns disappear; advanced conifers increase
Paleozoic	Permian	245 to 270	giant clubmosses decline; advanced conifers appear
	Carboniferous	270 to 350	coal-forming seed ferns and clubmosses dominate on land; primitive conifers evolve
	Devonian	350 to 400	early vascular plants (mosses and ferns) appear on land
	Silurian	400 to 440	algae dominate; first land plants appear
	Ordovician	440 to 500	algae dominate
	Cambrian	500 to 600	multicellular algae evolve
Proterozoic		600 to 1500	bacteria and simple algae present
Archeozoic		1500 to 4000	no fossils known; bacteria and unicellular algae may have been present

Table 23.1

2 Table 23.1 summarises the evolution of plants on Earth based on fossil records.

  a) Which geological era first provides definite fossil evidence of plant life on Earth? (1)

  b) i) To which group did the earliest known plants belong?
  ii) Is this group of plants now extinct? (2)

  c) i) During which geological period did vascular plants evolve?
  ii) What is meant by a vascular plant? (2)

  d) i) Identify TWO groups of vascular plants which have since become extinct according to the table.
  ii) Which of these contributed to Britain's coal deposits? (3)

  e) i) Which type of plant is now in decline and may be threatened with extinction in the future?
  ii) Give ONE reason why this is the case. (2)

3 Figure 23.2 shows a kite diagram which charts the abundance of species of five animal groups present on Earth over a timescale of 600 million years.

  a) i) Which animal group is thought to have been present on Earth approximately 600 million years ago?
  ii) Which group first appeared about 490 million years ago? (2)

  b) A wave of extinction occurred about 250 million years ago.

  i) Which animal group was reduced almost to extinction?
  ii) Which group was reduced but not seriously threatened?
  iii) Which group was completely wiped out? (3)

  c) Approximately when did
  i) the dinosaurs appear on Earth?
  ii) the mammals appear on Earth? (2)

  d) i) When did the dinosaurs become extinct?
  ii) What effect did this extinction have on the number of species of mammal present thereafter on Earth?
  iii) Give a possible explanation for the change in number of mammalian species over the last 60 million years. (3)

4 The sex of certain reptiles is known to be determined by the temperature at which their eggs are incubated. In the alligator, 30 °C produces females and 33 °C produces males. It is possible that this was also true of the dinosaurs. It is known that the end of the age of the dinosaurs coincided with a lowering of the Earth's temperature.

Based on the above information, construct an hypothesis to account for the extinction of the dinosaurs. (2)

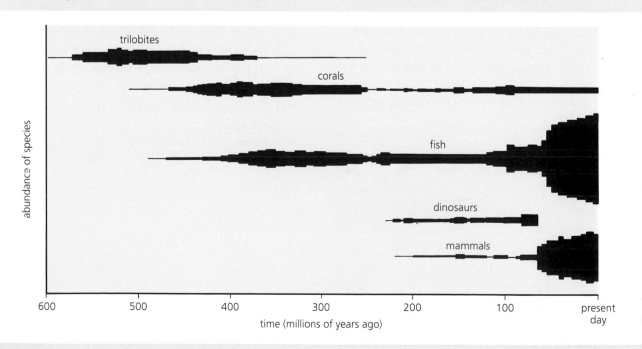

Figure 23.2

5 Several equal-sized areas of river bed from a non-polluted region and a polluted region were examined. The abundance of species for each area was recorded as shown in Table 23.3.

a) **i)** Do the two types of area differ in species richness?

ii) Explain your answer. (2)

Species	Mean number of individuals	
	Non-polluted	Polluted
rat-tailed maggot	2	21
sludge worm	3	29
mayfly nymph	15	0
caddisfly larva	11	0
stonefly nymph	12	0
freshwater mussel	7	0

Table 23.3

b) Calculate the biodiversity index for each area using the formula: (2)

$$D = \frac{N(N-1)}{\sum^n (n-1)}$$

where   D = biodiversity index
     N = total number of individuals of all species
     n = number of individuals per species
     $\sum$ = sum of

6 Every species of invertebrate living on each of the five small islands shown in Figure 23.3 was identified and recorded. No vertebrates were found on the islands. Next a tent was erected over each island and it was fumigated with pesticide to kill every animal. Recolonisation of the islands was then monitored over a period of a year. The results are shown in Table 23.4 where a tick indicates presence of a species.

Species	Island									
	1		2		3		4		5	
	b	a	b	a	b	a	b	a	b	a
A	✓			✓	✓	✓	✓	✓	✓	
B	✓	✓	✓	✓	✓			✓		✓
C						✓			✓	✓
D			✓			✓	✓	✓		
E						✓			✓	✓
F					✓	✓			✓	✓
G	✓	✓	✓					✓	✓	
H			✓			✓	✓		✓	✓	✓
I			✓	✓				✓	✓		✓
J	✓					✓	✓	✓	✓	✓	
K	✓	✓				✓		✓	✓		✓

(b = before fumigation, a = after fumigation)

Table 23.4

a) Do the data refer to the richness of species or relative abundance of species present on these islands? (1)

b) Which island possesses
i) the largest number of different species?
ii) the smallest number of different species?
iii) Suggest why this is the case. (3)

c) What effect did recolonisation have on the species equilibrium number of an island? (1)

d) Which island's species composition underwent
i) the least percentage change?
ii) the greatest percentage change? (2)

e) Following fumigation, which species managed to colonise
i) the most islands?
ii) the fewest islands? (2)

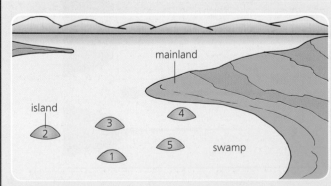

Figure 23.3

24 Threats to biodiversity

1 The data in Table 24.1 refer to the catch of plaice in the North Sea by a fleet of trawlers over a 5-year period.

a) Which age of plaice is the most common in each year's catch? (1)

b) i) What trend is shown by the data when read vertically downwards from 5-year-old fish?
ii) Explain why. (2)

c) Suggest why the '12+ years' entry is always greater than the '11 years' entry. (1)

d) Make a generalisation about the way in which the catch data for years 4 and 5 differ from those for years 1–3. (2)

e) The fishermen were pleased with their catch in years 4 and 5. Suggest why they should be concerned about the future (if the trend shown by the data continues). (2)

f) What is the percentage decline in number of 10-year-old fish in the 5-year study? (1)

2 Read the passage and answer the questions that follow it.

Butterflies are very sensitive to environmental change. The slightly warmer conditions that have occurred in the UK in recent years have favoured some species but not others. The fortunate ones are able to change their distribution in response to climate change. The **brown argus**, for example, has rapidly expanded its geographical range and the variety of flowering species upon which it feeds. However, the range occupied by the **silver-studded blue** has decreased significantly and the **chequered skipper** is confined to a few parts of Scotland, having vanished completely from England.

Some butterfly species are found to respond to climate change by moving their range. The **scotch argus**, for example, is found to be heading northwards while the **mountain ringlet** is moving its range to a higher altitude.

The rate at which a species of butterfly can change its range is affected by availability of suitable new habitats. Where a habitat has become severely fragmented by human activities, the ability of a species to track a shift in climate may be impeded by long stretches of unfavourable environment lying between one unspoiled habitat fragment and another.

a) i) Experts describe the brown argus butterfly as a *mobile generalist*. Justify this description using TWO pieces of information from the passage.
ii) Suggest why the silver-studded blue is described as a *habitat specialist*.
iii) Identify a butterfly from the passage that is probably extinct from England. (4)

Age of fish (years)	Total number of plaice caught				
	Year 1	Year 2	Year 3	Year 4	Year 5
2	89	78	83	421	573
3	547	625	602	2 127	2 268
4	2 485	2 331	2 491	2 683	2 594
5	2 137	2 027	2 076	1 527	1 332
6	891	766	750	363	257
7	417	389	428	215	209
8	235	201	217	92	76
9	67	94	86	41	38
10	50	81	63	20	15
11	43	57	38	17	12
12+	77	94	69	32	28

Table 24.1

b) Even when an area becomes warmer and suitable for occupancy by a particular species of butterfly, often that species is unable to extend its range into the new area. Suggest why. (2)

c) i) Explain why 'moving its range to a higher altitude' solves the mountain ringlet butterfly's problem.
ii) Why might this response to climatic change be disastrous in the long run? (2)

d) Suggest ONE human activity that could be responsible for '... *a habitat ... severely fragmented by human activities ...*' (1)

3 The data in Table 24.2 refer to estimated numbers of six species of whale. Calculate the data missing from boxes **a)–e)**. (5)

4 Read the passage and answer the questions that follow it.

The **zebra mussel** is a freshwater invertebrate with a yellow and brown striped shell that varies in length from 6 to 50 mm. It is native to Eastern European waters but was introduced to North America in the ballast water of freighters.

The female can produce several hundred thousand eggs per year. These become larvae that attach themselves to any firm surface and grow into adults. One such surface is the shell of the local species of mussel which dies and becomes extinct in the area affected.

Zebra mussels are now widespread in the USA and are responsible for blocking pipes and water intakes to hydroelectric schemes. Their shells are sharp enough to shear fishing lines and injure swimmers. They feed on plankton by filtering lake water, which increases its clarity and enables algae to grow at deeper depths.

Zebra mussels are of high nutritional value to their natural predators, crayfish and fish such as roach, common in Eastern European lakes. Zebra mussels are credited with increasing the population numbers of fish such as smallmouth bass and yellow perch in some American lakes.

a) i) Which of the following terms best describes the zebra mussel – *introduced*, *naturalised* or *invasive*?
ii) Justify your choice. (2)

b) Give an example of a way in which the spread of the zebra mussel in the USA has impacted negatively on:
i) recreational activities
ii) a utility. (2)

c) The filtering action of zebra mussels helps to remove pollutants from lake water.
i) Which member of the lake ecosystem benefits from this effect?
ii) Explain why. (2)

d) Name:
i) a vertebrate
ii) an invertebrate that is a natural predator of the zebra mussel in its native ecosystem. (2)

e) Suggest the means by which an attempt could be made to exert biological control of zebra mussels in a small lake in the USA. (1)

f) Does shell length in zebra mussels show discrete or continuous variation? (1)

5 Give an account of the threat to biodiversity under the following headings:

a) the bottleneck effect (3)

b) habitat fragmentation (3)

c) invasive species. (4)

Species of whale	Estimated number		Estimated percentage remaining
	Before commercial whaling	Present day	
Blue	200 000	5 000	2.50
Fin	450 000	33 000	**a)**
Humpback	**b)**	28 000	20.00
Right	50 000	**c)**	16.80
Sei	250 000	40 000	**d)**
Sperm	**e)**	360 000	24.00

Table 24.2

Answers

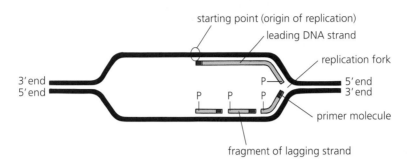

Figure An2.1

1 Structure of DNA

1 a) X = 22.0; Y = 0.98 (2)

b) (i) The number of adenine bases in DNA equals the number of thymine bases and the number of guanine bases equals the number of cytosine bases (A : T = 1:1 and G : C = 1:1).
(ii) Yes   **(iii)** Because the percentage of A is always very nearly equal to the percentage of T but not close to that of G or C. Similarly the percentage of G is always close to the percentage of C but not close to that of A or T. (3)

c) C (1)

2 a) 30% (1) **b)** 3200 (1)

3 a) (i) 1 = chromosome, 2 = DNA, 3 = base
(ii) 1   **(iii)** 3 (5)

b) (i) 10 000 : 1   **(ii)** Because this is a constant reliable measurement whereas length measured in μm varies according to degree of coiling. (2)

4 a) When the DNA strands become reunited, some containing ^{14}N pair with others containing ^{14}N, some ^{14}N combine with ^{15}N and some ^{15}N combine with ^{15}N. This produces three distinct marker bands. (2)

b) When the DNA strands become reunited, those of virus 1 are not complementary to those of virus 2 so no 'hybrid' ^{14}N + ^{15}N DNA double helices can be formed. (2)

c) *E.coli* host cells could be grown in ^{15}N as their only source of nitrogen for many generations. They could then be infected with bacteriophage virus which would take up ^{15}N in the copies that it made of itself. (3)

2 Replication of DNA

1 a) See Figure An2.1 (6)

b) (i) 20 000 minutes   **(ii)** During replication, many replication forks operate simultaneously which ensures speedy copying of the DNA. (2)

2 a) (i) Semi-logarithmic   **(ii)** To accommodate the very high numbers involved. (2)

b) 23 (1)

c) 10 (1)

d) (i) 1 000 000 000   **(ii)** One billion (2)

3 See core text pages 19–22. (9)

3 Control of gene expression

1 (1)

N	AAρ	AArn	AAſ	AArn	AAs	AAd	AAe	AAe	AAſ	AAj

Figure An3.1

2 a) X = phenylalanine, Y = threonine, Z = lysine (3)

b) (i) X   **(ii)** Z   **(iii)** The most soluble one is carried to the highest position by the solvent. (2)

3 a) (i) Lower molecular weight   **(ii)** This is suggested by the fact that they have travelled the greatest distance from the negative electrode. (2)

b) (i) Alpha-2-globulins   **(ii)** Iron-deficiency anaemia (2)

c) **(i)** D   **(ii)** Because gamma-globulins also increase in concentration for other reasons such as a response to viral invasion. (2)

4 a) Casein contains them all. Group 2 rats gained weight throughout the experiment. Zein lacks two essential amino acids. Group 1 rats lost weight throughout the experiment. (4)

b) **(i)** Zein   **(ii)** Their diet could have been changed to casein or to zein supplemented with the two essential amino acids that it lacks. (3)

c) 35 g (1)

d) 20% (1)

5 a) = 2

b) = 4

c) = 1

d) = 3 (3)

6 a) The increase in relative numbers of ribosomes in cells during day 1 to 5 indicates that this is the period of most rapid protein synthesis and growth of the new leaf. After day 5 growth slows down and eventually comes to a halt at day 11 when the leaf has reached its full size. (2)

b) A basic number of ribosomes will always be needed by a cell of a fully grown leaf to make proteins such as enzymes essential for biochemical pathways (e.g. photosynthesis). (1)

7 a) 1 = C, 2 = T, 3 = T, 4 = A, 5 = U, 6 = A, 7 = G, 8 = C, 9 = G (2)

b) P = transcription and release of mRNA; Q = translation of mRNA into protein (1)

c) See Table An3.1 (2)

d) CAA (1)

e) U = proline, V = glutamine, W = glutamic acid, X = cysteine, Y = arginine, Z = isoleucine (2)

f) **(i)** ACACUUGCGGGC
(ii) TGTGAACGCCCG (2)

8 See core text pages 38–41. (9)

Amino acid	Codon	Anticodon
alanine	**GCG**	CGC
arginine	CGC	**GCG**
cysteine	**UGU**	ACA
glutamic acid	GAA	**CUU**
glutamine	**CAA**	GUU
glycine	GGC	**CCG**
isoleucine	**AUA**	UAU
leucine	CUU	**GAA**
proline	**CCG**	GGC
threonine	ACA	**UGU**
tyrosine	**UAU**	AUA
valine	GUU	**CAA**

Table An3.1

4 Cellular differentiation

1 a) Q, S, P, T, R (1)

b) P, Q, S and T (1)

c) **(i)** R   **(ii)** It is a hollow tube lined with lignin. **(iii)** A hollow tube is suited to water transport and lignin provides the tube with support. (5)

2 a) Lateral (1)

b) 8 years (1)

c) Year 4 (1)

d) **(i)** Year 6   **(ii)** This is the narrowest ring indicating poorest growth because infected leaves sent less food than normal to the cambium. (2)

3 a) = 3,   **b)** =1,   **c)** = 5,   **d)** = 2, **e)** = 4 (4)

4 W = zygote, X = embryonic stem cell, Y = tissue (adult) stem cell, Z = specialised cell (3)

5 a) Nuclear transfer technique (1)

b) Because she is a genetic copy of another sheep. (1)

c) **(i)** White   **(ii)** Because her genetic material came from a white-faced sheep. (2)

d) **(i)** A   **(ii)** The DNA that she received came from a sheep not a ram. Therefore she could not have received a Y chromosome necessary to become a male. (2)

6 a) **(i)** B, C, E, G, J   **(ii)** A, D, F, H, I (2)

b) Open-ended answer which depends on the reader's personal opinion.

7 a) Jill (1)

b) (i) Unconvincing   **(ii)** Because some embryos are lost naturally, does not justify using embryos for stem cell research. (2)

8 See core text pages 49–50. (9)

5 Structure of the genome

1 a) A = mRNA, B = rRNA, C = tRNA (3)

b) W (1)

c) (i) = 2   **(ii)** = 4   **(iii)** = 1   **(iv)** = 3 (3)

2 A, D, C, E, B (1)

6 Mutations

1 a) Deletion

b) Substitution

c) Insertion (3)

2 a) (i) Mean root length   **(ii)** Radiation dosage (1)

b) (4)

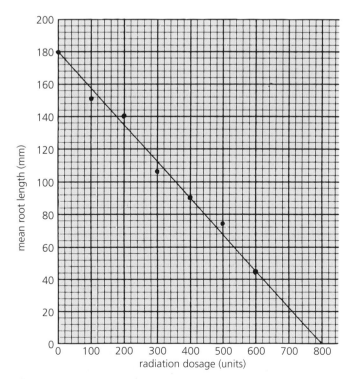

Figure An6.1

c) (i) An inverse relationship   **(ii)** Radiation damages the cells and their genetic material. The greater the dose of radiation, the worse the damage inflicted. (2)

d) 800 units (1)

e) To increase the reliability of the results (1)

f) 500 (mutations at gene site per million gametes) (1)

3 Thousands of years ago when all humans were *hunter-gatherers*, adults had no post-weaning tolerance for lactose. However, among some humans in Europe who had become *early dairy farmers*, a *point mutation* arose that kept the *lactose-coding gene* switched on after weaning. This gave the people who inherited the mutant gene a *selective advantage* because they could eat plenty of dairy products without becoming ill. A high percentage of European Americans and European Australians are lactose tolerant because they are descendents of the mutant Europeans. The Inuit and the Australian Aborigines have no lactose tolerance because they have descended from hunter-gatherers. (5)

4 a) (i)

original cross	HH	X	HS
gametes	all H		H and S
F$_1$ generation	HH and HS		

Figure An6.2

(ii) (4)

original cross	HS	X	HS
gametes	H and S		H and S
F$_1$ generation	HH, HS, HS, SS		

Figure An6.3

b) A higher percentage of local people in malarial areas have sickle-cell trait; they are resistant to malaria and are favoured by natural selection. This selective advantage is lost in non-malarial areas therefore the percentage of sickle-cell trait sufferers is very low. (2)

5 a) Cell 1 = deletion; Cell 2 = duplication (2)

b) (i) Cell 1   **(ii)** Essential genes would probably have been lost. (2)

6 a) (i) = Y   **(ii)** = X (1)

b) (i) Y   **(ii)** TUV (2)

7 a) (i) A   **(ii)** BB   **(iii)** AB   **(iv)** AB (2)

b) Because the chromosomes in genomes A and B are unable to pair up properly during gamete formation. (1)

c) A further error occurred during the separation of chromosomes at cell division and the AB genomes became AABB. (2)

d) (i) AA (or BB) (ii) AABB (iii) Because they normally show an increase in size and vigour compared to their diploid relatives. (3)

8 See core text pages 60–62. (10)

7 Evolution

1 a) Vertical (1)

b) (3)

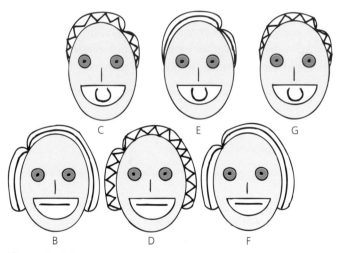

Figure An7.1

2 a) The black one (1)

b) (i)

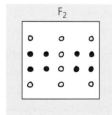

Figure An7.2

(ii) 1 : 1 (2)

c)

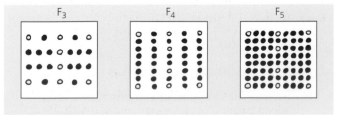

Figure An7.3

(i) F_3 (ii) F_5 (2)

3 a) Consumption of warfarin interferes with the blood-clotting mechanism and the rat bleeds to death if it becomes cut or injured. (1)

b) It thins their blood and prevents the formation of unwanted internal clots. (1)

c) Mutation (1)

d) It has been favoured by natural selection since members of the sensitive strain normally die after eating the warfarin. (1)

e) Extinction (1)

f) Very few $W^r W^r$ rats will be fortunate enough to find a continuous supply of food containing the large amount of vitamin K that they need. (2)

4 a) (4)

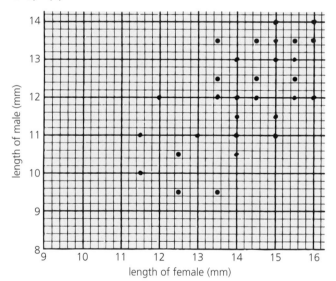

Figure An7.4

b) Larger males tend to mate with larger females. (1)

c) (i) Pair 17 (ii) Pair 11 (iii) It may be the case that animals smaller than this were unable to attract a mate since brine shrimps (regardless of their own individual size) are attracted to larger shrimps as potential mates. (3)

5 a) To increase the reliability of the results (1)

b) (i) 290 mm (ii) 120 mm (iii) As tail length increases so does the number of active nests per male bird's territory. (3)

c) If mates with the best characteristics are chosen most often, these characteristics will have the best chance of being inherited by members of the next generation. (2)

d) (i) Engaging in a contest to secure a territory
(ii) Choosing a mate based on the length of his tail (2)

e) (i) The number of active nests would increase.
(ii) The longer tail might make the birds more easily caught by predators. The production of such long tail feathers every year might be too costly in food resources. (3)

6 a) 1 is allopatric because the barrier is geographical (a river). 2 is sympatric because the new species lives among the original one but is reproductively isolated from it by polyploidy. (4)

b) A cross could be attempted between the two populations using several members of each type to see if they could produce fertile offspring. (2)

7 a) Quantitative = body length (or tail length); qualitative = ventral colour (or presence or absence of pectoral spot) (2)

b) They are able to interbreed and produce fertile offspring. (1)

c) The genetic distance between this type of mouse and the one in Norway is much less than that between this mouse and the one on the Scottish mainland suggesting that the ancestor was Norse. (1)

d) (i) It lends support to Berry.   (ii) After the Ice Age, when *Apodemus* returned to the Scottish mainland (probably from southern parts of the UK following repopulation), a barrier of water separated the mainland from the Shetlands. Therefore the route from Norway seems more likely. (2)

e) If *A. s. fridariensis* on Fair Isle did arise from *A. s. granti* from Yell then the difference in their genetic distances can be explained as follows. The colonisers from Yell comprised a small splinter group of which the members were genetically atypical of *A. s. granti* as a whole. This group eventually gave rise to a population with some gene frequencies very different from their Yell ancestors (i.e. the founder effect). (2)

f) A common ancestor could have spread throughout the islands along with the human inhabitants in olden times when conditions were primitive. Different groups of mice have been kept isolated by water barriers ever since and have started to take different courses of evolution in isolation (but not enough time has elapsed yet for complete speciation to have occurred). (2)

8 a) (i) 1   (ii) Gene flow is possible from A to F via hybrid zones. (2)

b) (i) 2   (ii) 3   (iii) 1 (3)

9 See core text pages 85–86. (9)

8 Genomic sequencing

1 AACCGATCAGCGCAGCGCTTGATCAGATCGCGCTAG (1)

2 a) No

b) These SNPs might both be neutral mutations that have no effect on the protein that is coded. (2)

3 a) (i) It is a variation in DNA sequence that affects a single base pair in a DNA chain.   (ii) Site 4 (2)

b) 5 (1)

c) (i) 7 and 12   (ii) 5 and 9   (iii) 8 (3)

d) 17 (1)

e) (i) CTTATG   (ii) 45% (2)

f) 10 (1)

g) 4 and 11 (1)

h) Increase the number of people sampled and include more sites in the study. (2)

4 a) (i) Neuron   (ii) Common ancestor
(iii) Mutation   (iv) Transcription factor
(v) Natural selection (5)

b) HAR1 gene in chimpanzees lacks the 18 base-pair substitutions that are present in the human version of the gene. FOXP2 gene in chimpanzees has two substitutions that are absent in the human version of the gene. (2)

c) It is possible that the version of HAR1 gene present in humans has contributed to improved development of a part of the brain responsible for intelligence. (1)

d) Substitution (1)

e) Their FOXP2 protein differs from that of humans by two amino acids. Perhaps it is unable to attach itself to and regulate the gene(s) needed for the development of the neural circuits that make speech possible. (2)

f) It would seem that the HAR1 gene helps to make humans more intelligent and that the FOXP2 gene allows them to communicate using speech. So in each case, the gene confers an advantage that helps them to survive. Therefore humans with these genes tend to be selected in the struggle for survival. (2)

5 a) Fish and reptiles (1)

b) (i) Vertebrates and insects **(ii)** 600 million years ago (2)

c) (i) Mammals **(ii)** When their cytochrome c is compared, more differences exist between mammals and reptiles than between birds and reptiles suggesting that mammals diverged earlier from reptiles than birds. (2)

d) Fish and amphibian specimens could have their cytochrome c compared and the number of differences found in their amino acids could be used to work out from the graph their probable point of divergence. (2)

6 a) (i) 39 996 **(ii)** 8322 **(iii)** 1.23 : 1 (3)

b) *Bradyrhizobium japonicum* (1)

c) (i) *Neurospora crassa* **(ii)** Its genome is 'gene sparse' compared with the other two so the spaces between the protein-coding genes probably contain a large amount of repetitive DNA. (2)

d) 1 = Eukaryotes because it has a nucleus with a double membrane. 2 = Bacteria because it has no introns. 3 = Archaea because it has few introns but no nuclear membrane. (3)

7 a) (i) 10^7 m **(ii)** 10^4 km; ten thousand kilometres (2)

b) (i) No **(ii)** It is based on the genomes of several people. (2)

8 a) (4)

Alleles of gene present in genome	State of enzyme	Person's metabolic profile
two null alleles	non-functional	**poor**
one null allele and one inferior allele	**partly functional**	**intermediate**
one or two normal alleles	**fully functional**	extensive
more than two copies of normal allele	highly functional	**ultra-rapid**

Table An8.1

b) Duplication (1)

c) (i) Poor metabolisers **(ii)** Their bodies will be so slow to clear the drug that it may do them harm. (2)

d) (i) Ultra-rapid metabolisers **(ii)** Their bodies

would remove the drug so quickly that it would not have time to bring about the desired effect. (2)

e) If the personal genome sequencing becomes routine then knowledge of a person's DNA profile may enable doctors to customise medical treatments to suit an individual's exact requirements. (2)

9 Metabolic pathways and their control

1 a) (i) 5 **(ii)** 3 (2)

b) Some of I would be converted to G by enzyme 5 and then G would be converted to H by enzyme 4. (2)

c) (i) H could become L and M by the action of enzyme 8 and then L and M could become J and K by the action of enzyme 7.
(ii) $H + I \xrightarrow{\text{enzyme 6}} J + K \xrightarrow{\text{enzyme 7}} L + M$
(iii) $G \xrightarrow{\text{enzyme 4}} H \xrightarrow{\text{enzyme 8}} L + M \xrightarrow{\text{enzyme 7}} J + K \xrightarrow{\text{enzyme 6}} H + I$ (3)

d) It allows finely-tuned control and prevents build-ups and bottlenecks. (1)

2 a) (i) 4 **(ii)** 3 **(iii)** 1 **(iv)** 2 (3)

b) The pumping of H^+ ions into a lysosome to maintain the low pH inside (2)

c) (3)

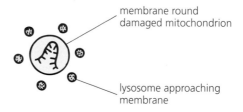

membrane round damaged mitochondrion

lysosome approaching membrane

Figure An9.1

d) The cells are programmed to die at a certain stage of embryonic development and then lysosomes digest and remove them. (1)

e) They are recycled for use in the frog's body after lysosomes have broken the cells down. (1)

3 a) (i) Outside **(ii)** Inside **(iii)** Inside **(iv)** Outside **(v)** The sodium/potassium pump actively transports sodium to the outside and potassium to the inside. (3)

b) 55 times (1)

c) (i) Brings about an increase
(ii) Sugar, needed for energy, has become a limiting factor.

(iii) Inverse relationship; energy is needed for ion uptake, therefore as ions are taken up, the number of units of sugar present decreases. (4)

4 a) P and S (1)

b) (i) Q, S, P, R   **(ii)** R, P, S, Q (2)

5 a) See Figure An9.2 (3)

b) Enzyme concentration (1)

c) (i) 6 molecules per unit time   **(ii)** All the enzyme's active sites were occupied.   **(iii)** 1 and 2 (3)

6 a) See core text pages 123–124. (3)

b) See core text page 122. (3)

c) See core text page 124. (3)

7 B (1)

8 a) (i),   (ii) and   **(iii)** See Figure An8.1 (4)

b) A (1)

c) 3 times (1)

d) (i) 61.54%   **(ii)** 10% (2)

e) There would always be a few enzyme sites blocked by inhibitor. (1)

9 a) (i) =Y,   **(ii)** = Z,   **(iii)** = X (2)

b) X (1)

c) X, Y and Z (1)

d) Non-competitive (1)

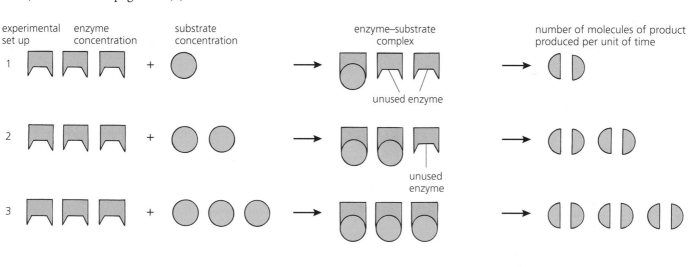

Figure An9.2

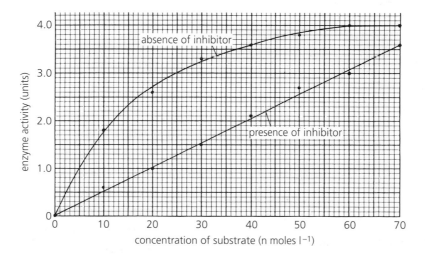

Figure An9.3

10 a) 1, 2 and 3 (1)

b) Substrate concentration (1)

c) 4, 5 and 6 (1)

d) Experiment = 4, 5 and 6; controls = 1, 2 and 3 (2)

e) **(i)** Iodine solution   **(ii)** Non-competitively
(iii) If it had been a competitive inhibitor, the
inhibitory effect would have decreased as substrate
concentration increased and this would have resulted
in some yellow colour appearing in tube 6 and maybe
a faint yellow colour in tube 5. However, iodine
completely inhibited the enzyme at all
concentrations of ONPG showing that it acted
non-competitively. (4)

11 a) **(i)** Carbamyl phosphate and aspartate
(ii) Carbamyl aspartate and phosphate
(iii) Cytidylic acid (3)

b) **(i)** The concentration of carbamyl phosphate will
increase.   **(ii)** Fewer molecules of P will be free to
act on carbamyl phosphate. (2)

c) **(i)** Decreased   **(ii)** There will be so little cytidylic
acid present that very few molecules of enzyme P will
be affected by the negative feedback process. (2)

d) All three (1)

12 See core text pages 132–136. (10)

10 Cellular respiration

1 a) and **b)** (4)

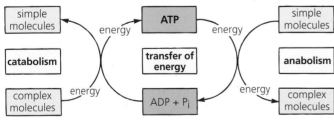

Figure An10.1

2 a) C

b) A

c) C

d) C

e) A (5)

3 a) 56% (1)

b) 1267.2 kJ (1)

c) Synthesis of protein from amino acids; contraction of
muscles (2)

4 a) (5)

Stage of respiratory pathway	Principal reaction or process that occurs	Products
glycolysis	splitting of glucose into [pyruvate]	[ATP], NADH and pyruvate
[citric] acid cycle	removal of [hydrogen] ions from molecules of respiratory [substrate]	[CO_2], $FADH_2$, [NADH] and ATP
[electron] transport chain	release of [energy] to form ATP	ATP and [water]

Table An10.1

b) Glycolysis (1)

c) Electron transport chain (1)

d) Glycolysis and citric acid cycle (2)

e) Citric acid cycle and electron transport chain (2)

5 a) **(i)** Intermembrane space   **(ii)** A flow of
high-energy electrons from NADH and $FADH_2$
pumps H^+ ions across the membrane against a
concentration gradient. (3)

b) **(i)** ATP synthase   **(ii)** The return flow of H^+
ions to the region of lower H^+ ion concentration via
molecule X makes part of it rotate and catalyse the
synthesis of ATP. (3)

c) By stopping electron flow, cyanide brings the
movement of H^+ ions to a halt therefore no ATP is
synthesised and the organism lacks access to energy
and dies. (2)

6 a) See Figure An10.2 (4)

b) **(i)** The result at 70 min   **(ii)** It is much lower
than would be expected from the general trend. (2)

c) 6400% (1)

d) It is able to make very good use of glucose but not
able to make good use of galactose or lactose. (1)

e) **(i)** It is hardly able to break lactose down.
(ii) If it had been able to do so, glucose would have
been released from lactose and rapidly used as a
respiratory substrate. (2)

f) Repeat the experiment (1)

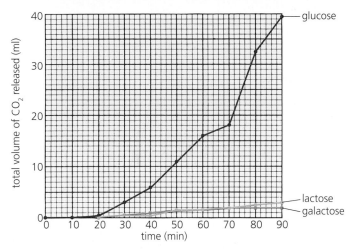

Figure An10.2

g) It would have digested lactose to glucose and galactose therefore the lactose flask would have worked as well as the original flask containing glucose. There would have been no effect in the galactose flask. The flask containing glucose would work as well as, but no better than, before. (2)

7 a) D (1)

b) B (1)

c) (i) Yes   **(ii)** Because excess carbohydrate can go route IDB or IKMEB to fat. (3)

d) They can break down stores of fat (and eventually tissue protein) to obtain energy after they have exhausted their supply of glycogen. (2)

8 a) Production of ATP (1)

b) ADP (1)

c) (i) It increased.   **(ii)** The process of respiration (which releases CO_2) was no longer limited by shortage of inorganic phosphate to make ATP. (2)

d) Ethanol (formed during fermentation) began to poison some of the yeast cells. (1)

11 Metabolic rate

1 a) BMR is lower in females. BMR decreases with age. (2)

b) 1.5 times (1)

c) 27.78% (1)

2 a) (i) TSA = 2400 cm², TV = 8000 cm³
   (ii) TSA = 4800 cm², TV = 8000 cm³ (2)

b) (i) 0.3 : 1   **(ii)** 0.6 : 1 (2)

c) Small cube (1)

d) (i) A   **(ii)** F (1)

e) (i) F   **(ii)** A (1)

f) (i) The smaller the body size, the higher the metabolic rate and vice versa.   **(ii)** The smallest animal needs the highest metabolic rate because it has the largest surface area relative to its body size from which heat can be lost. (2)

3 a) See Table An11.1 (5)

b) (i) Incomplete double   **(ii)** Frog
   (iii) A = high, B = low, C = low (5)

4 a) (i) 0 m   **(ii)** 5300 m (2)

b) (i) 4.2   **(ii)** 6.1 (2)

c) (i) 78   **(ii)** 6.4 (2)

d) (i) They show the same trend. As altitude increases, so does red blood cell number.   **(ii)** Extra oxygen is needed at higher altitudes where the air is thinner. (2)

e) 66 days (1)

f) (i) Red blood corpuscle count lags behind altitude.   **(ii)** Time is needed by the body to respond to the higher altitude. (2)

g) They will have a higher number of red blood corpuscles and therefore more oxygen available for aerobic respiration and energy release. (2)

Vertebrate group	Type of circulation	Number of chambers in heart	Pressure of blood arriving at skeletal muscles	Evolutionary level of circulatory system
fish	single	2	low	primitive
amphibian/reptile	incomplete double	3	high	intermediate
mammal	complete double	4	high	advanced

Table An11.1

12 Metabolism in conformers and regulators

1 a) (i) 30°C   (ii) 32°C (1)

  b) (i) 23°C   (ii) 30°C (1)

  c) (i) Y   (ii) X (1)

  d) (i) X   (ii) Behavioural (2)

  e) If members of population Y sought one of the rare sunny spots in the forest they would run the risk of:

    (i) expending more energy in movement than they would gain from the sun and

    (ii) increasing their chance of being caught by a predator. (2)

2 a) Hypothalamus (1)

  b) It sends nerve impulses to them. (1)

  c) (i) It would become constricted.   (ii) Less blood would flow to the skin surface so less heat would be lost by radiation. (2)

  d) (i) It would increase its rate of sweat production. (ii) When the liquid sweat coated the outside of the skin, excess body heat would be used to convert it to water vapour thereby cooling the body. (2)

3 a) See Figure An12.1 (3) and b) See Figure An12.1 (4)

  c) (i) Increase   (ii) Decrease   (iii) Time is required for heat gain or loss by tissues to affect blood temperature. (3)

  d) (i) Vasodilation has occurred.   (ii) Overheating of the body is corrected by excess heat being lost by radiation from extra blood at the skin surface. (2)

  e) (i) D   (ii) Overcooling of the body is corrected by the heat generated by muscular contraction. (2)

4 See core text pages 166–170. (9)

13 Metabolism and adverse conditions

1 a) See Figure An13.1 (5)

  b) If 75% or more germinated (and developed a root) (1)

  c) Dry and cold (2)

2 a) 16 times (1)

  b) $1.2\,kJ\,m^{-2}\,min^{-1}$ (1)

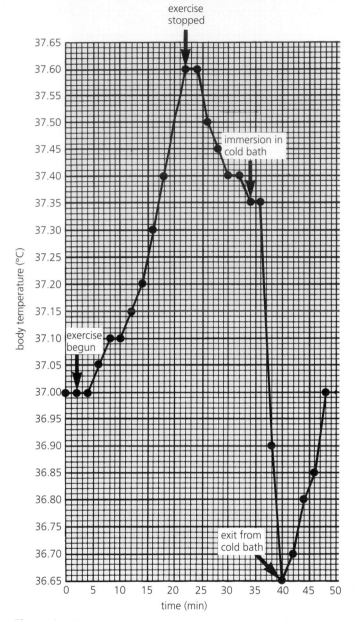

Figure An12.1

  c) 130 times (1)

  d) 91.67 (1)

3 a) No germination (1)

  b) A dish containing seeds free of gel (1)

  c) Replicate plates should have been set up. (1)

  d) The juicy gel could be separated from the seeds of the Scottish tomatoes and used to soak blotting paper in several sterile Petri dishes. South American tomato seeds that have been separated from their own gel and washed could be added to these dishes and incubated to find out whether or not they germinate. (3)

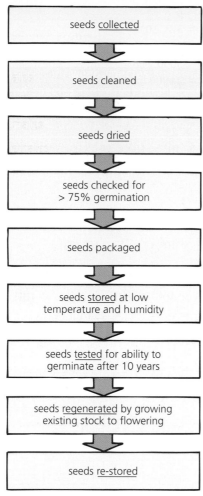

Figure An13.1

e) **(i)** Dormancy-breaking experiments
(ii) If they are not tested for dormancy, they might be thought of as dead and be discarded in error. (2)

4 a) (5)

Feature	European hedgehog	Desert hedgehog
habitat	wooded area	edge of desert
food source	earthworms and insects	scorpions and snakes
time of dormancy	winter	summer
type of dormancy	hibernation	aestivation
extent of drop in metabolic rate	large	small
relative number of times animal wakes up during dormancy	few	many

Table An13.1

b) Relatively more heat is lost by an animal with a smaller body size and large thin extremities which makes the desert hedgehog perfectly adapted to survival in the desert. (2)

c) **(i)** European   **(ii)** It needs this fat to act as insulation and to generate energy, enabling it to survive lengthy periods of extreme cold when food is scarce. (3)

5 a) C, F, H, A, D, G, B, E (1)

b) S/he would hold it round the body (not round the head or wings), put it in a bag and fix the band to its leg using special pliers back in the laboratory. (3)

c) Their migratory routes and where they spend the summer and winter. (1)

6 a) It increases (1)

b) **(i)** A minimum of 14 hours of light in each 24-hour cycle   **(ii)** Mid-April (2)

c) They had not been exposed to the length of photoperiod that triggers this behaviour until mid-May. (1)

d) Because birds received 12 hours of light in mid-March but there was no response. (1)

7 a) Q (1)

b) **(i)** Inherited   **(ii)** P and S (2)

c) R (1)

d) They were young birds that had not flown the route before and were not able to recognise familiar geographical features to help them alter their course towards the correct destination. (2)

8 (1) cells arranged singly or as short chains ....
go to (2)

cells arranged in long chains ....
go to (3)

(2) cells rod-shaped ....
Chlorobium

cells egg-shaped ....
Prosthecochloris

(3) vacuoles present ....
Pelodictyon

vacuoles absent ....
Clathrochloris (3)

9 See core text pages 179–180. (9)

14 Environmental control of metabolism

1 a) A = cell wall, B = cell membrane, C = vacuole, D = nucleus, E = mitochondrion (5)

b) This filamentous fungus is a **multicellular** member of the **eukaryotes**. (2)

c) **(i)** 8×10^{-3} **(ii)** 8×10^{-6} (2)

2 a) D (1)

b) A – The air-in tube lacks a filter/the end of the air-out tube is immersed in solution.

B – The end of the tube from the syringe for taking samples is not immersed in the solution.

C – The air-in and air-out tubes are the wrong way round and one tube lacks a filter. (3)

3 a) **(i)** A   **(ii)** It follows the normal growth pattern and eventually the cells die at 15 hours once a high concentration of alcohol builds up. (2)

b) **(i)** C   **(ii)** It continues to decrease as it is used up by the yeast cells. (2)

c) **(i)** B   **(ii)** It does not appear for a few hours until the yeast has passed its lag phase. It levels off once the yeast cells go into decline. (2)

4 a) (4)

Time (in 20-minute intervals)	Cell number ($\times 10^3$)	Cell number (correct to two decimal places)
0	3	3.00×10^3
1	6	6.00×10^3
2	12	1.20×10^4
3	24	2.40×10^4
4	48	4.80×10^4
5	96	9.60×10^4
6	192	1.92×10^5
7	384	3.84×10^5
8	768	7.68×10^5
9	1536	1.54×10^6
10	3072	3.07×10^6
11	6144	6.14×10^6
12	12 288	1.23×10^7

Table An14.1

b) 3 h 20 min (1)

5 a) **(i)** $q = p \times 2^n$
$$= 3 \times 10^3 \times 2^n$$
$$= 3000 \times 2^3$$
$$= 3000 \times 8$$
$$= 24\,000 \text{ bacteria}$$

(ii) $g = {}^t/_n = {}^{60}/_3 = 20$ min (2)

b) $q = p \times 2^n$
$$\therefore 16 \times 10^3 = 10^3 \times 2^n$$
$$\therefore 16 = 2^n$$
$$\therefore 2^4 = 2^n$$
$$\therefore n = 4$$
$$g = {}^t/_n = {}^{120}/_4 = 30 \text{ min (2)}$$

6 a) $P = 8 \times 10^6$, $Q = 1 \times 10^6$ (2)

b) **(i)** 16×10^6 **(ii)** 16 million (2)

c) **(i)** 28×10^6 **(ii)** 32 times   **(iii)** 45 min
(iv) $g = {}^t/_n = {}^{225}/_5 = 45$ min (4)

7 a) and **b)** (6)

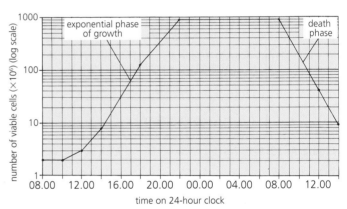

Figure An14.1

c) 30 (1)

d) **(i)** 22.00–08.00   **(ii)** The number of cells may have varied during this 10-hour period when no readings were taken.   **(iii)** Take more readings e.g. every 2 hours (3)

8 a) Cleaning of metals, electroplating, flavouring (1)

b) **(i)** Prevention of onward metabolism of citrate round the citric acid cycle. Lack of oxaloacetate for the formation of citric acid. Inhibition of phosphofructokinase by high concentrations of citric acid exerting negative feedback control.
(ii) Lack of oxaloacetate did not occur because a different pathway opened up.
(iii) Removal of iron prevents an enzyme converting citric acid to the next metabolite in the cycle. Addition of ammonium ions

counteracted the inhibiting effect of citric acid on phosphofructokinase. (6)

c) **(i)** The fermentation must be highly aerated.
(ii) This would supply the oxygen needed for aerobic respiration. (2)

d) To provide optimum conditions for enzymes to act. (1)

e) Nitrogen (1)

f) **(i)** 12.5 g/m³ per minute **(ii)** $12.5\,\mathrm{g\,m^{-3}\,min^{-1}}$ (2)

9 See core text pages 196–198. (9)

15 Genetic control of metabolism

1 a) (i) Mutations (%) **(ii)** Dosage of X-rays (2)

b) As the dosage of X-rays increases so does the percentage of mutations. (1)

c) **(i)** C **(ii)** B (2)

d) There is a good chance that the site-specific mutation will bring about the exact improvement required. The random nature of exposing the culture to a mutagen makes the chance of creating a strain with the desired property very remote. (2)

e) 0.1 per million cells (1)

2 a) See Figure An15.1 (4) and **b)** See Figure An15.1 (1)

3 a) 1 = B, 2 = D, 3 = E, 4 = C, 5 = A (4)

b) E (1)

c) **(i)** During transformation the bacterial cell takes up a piece of DNA from its surroundings and incorporates it into its DNA without a virus being involved. **(ii)** Horizontal (3)

4 a) B, D, F, E, A, C (1)

b) **(i)** B and D **(ii)** So that the cut ends would be compatible and stick together. (3)

c) F (1)

5 a) (i) Y **(ii)** X (1)

b) **(i)** 5 hours **(ii)** 2 hours after injection (1)

c) 20 hours (1)

d) The original biosynthetic insulin is slow to start acting and stops after 20 hours whereas X takes effect immediately and Y lasts a full 24 hours. (2)

6 See core text pages 209–211. (9)

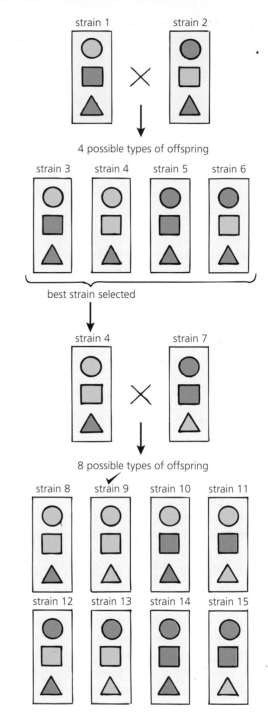

Figure An15.1

16 Ethical considerations in the use of microorganisms

1 a) Phase I used many healthy people who were paid. Phase II used a few asthma sufferers who were not paid. (3)

b) So that any improvements shown by sufferers receiving Q can be attributed to Q if the same improvements are not shown by the members of the control group. (2)

c) The results of phase III showed that patients on Q suffered fewer asthma attacks and used their dilators less often than the control group. (2)

d) **(i)** An inactive copy of the drug
(ii) They had gained a psychological benefit from taking the placebo which made their condition improve. (2)

e) **(i)** An addition   **(ii)** Although the condition of many sufferers improved, less than half were able to give up inhaled steroids. (2)

f) On average, elderly people's health is poorer than that of young people so a new untried drug might affect them adversely. Elderly people use so many medications that the data produced could be unreliable. (2)

2 a) **(i)** High   **(ii)** High   **(iii)** Z (3)

b) **(i)** Moderate   **(ii)** Low   **(iii)** X (3)

c) **(i)** 2   **(ii)** 3 (2)

d) 5 (1)

e) Containment of a risk 4 (but not risk 3) microbe must include controlled negative air pressure and presence of air locks and a compulsory shower for staff. (2)

17 Food supply, plant growth and productivity

1 Since the start of the green revolution, per-capita food production in Asia has continued to increase and has always been greater than that of the world average. Over the same timescale per-capita food production in Africa has always been less than that of the world average. (2)

2 a) 3 (1)

b) 6 (1)

c) 4 (1)

d) 6 (1)

3 a) W (1)

b) 4% (1)

c) Heat lost from the body. Energy used for movement. (2)

d) Faeces and urine contain chemical substances that provide energy for decomposers. (1)

e) 9.6 kJ (1)

4 a) 1 (1)

b) Any course of action that involves keeping the hen alive would be less successful than course 1 because it would involve feeding wheat to the hen. This would lead to a loss of energy at two links in the food chain whereas the man eating all the wheat would lead to energy being lost at only one link. (2)

5 a) 0.5 (1)

b) (1)

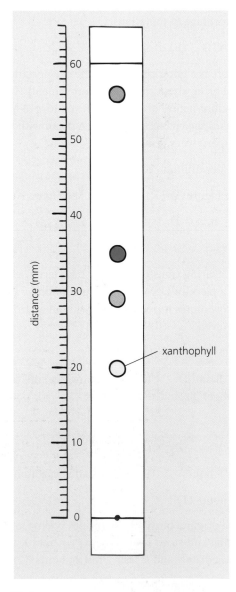

Figure An17.1

c) Carotene; 0.95 (2)

d) To produce a concentrated spot of pigments (1)

e) To prevent pigments from dissolving in the main bulk of the solvent at the bottom of the tube. (1)

f) Propanone (1)

6 a) Colour/wavelength of light (1)

b) They are absorbed by the filter. (1)

c) To make the results more reliable (1)

d) To allow the plant to return to equilibrium (1)

e) (2)

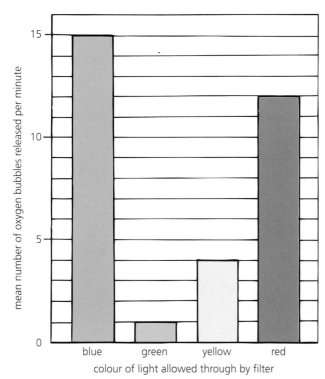

Figure An17.2

f) Photosynthetic rate was greatest in the blue light. (1)

g) (3)

Unit of length	Abbreviation	Fraction of one metre
metre	m	1
millimetre	mm	10^{-3}
micrometre	μm	10^{-6}
nanometre	nm	10^{-9}

Table An17.1

7 a) Chlorophyll a and b (2)

b) (i) Carotene and xanthophyll   **(ii)** Yes
(iii) In this case it accounts for the difference between the action spectrum (rate of photosynthesis at different light wavelengths) and absorption spectrum (percentage of light absorbed by chlorophyll at different light wavelengths). (4)

8 a) Blue and red (2)

b) Most photosynthesis occurs at these regions on the strand of alga. These sites therefore release most oxygen which in turn attracts many aerobic bacteria. (2)

9

◆ Grind up equal masses of both leaf types in sand and propanone.

◆ Filter to give two pigment extracts.

◆ Repeatedly spot and dry each extract onto its own thin layer strip or length of chromatography paper.

◆ Add appropriate solvent (e.g. propanone, cyclohexane and petroleum ether) to two boiling tubes and run the two chromatograms by allowing the solvent to ascend the paper or strips.

◆ Stop the process when the solvent is close to the top of the papers or strips and mark the solvent front on each in pencil.

◆ Calculate Rf values for all the pigment spots.

◆ Compare the chromatograms and find out whether the arrangement and number of pigments and their Rf values differ or not. (10)

10 a)–g) (6)

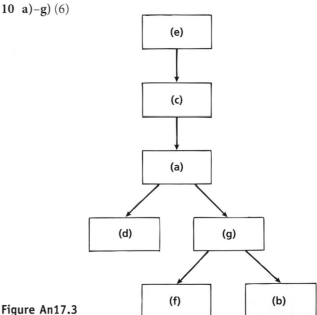

Figure An17.3

11 a) (2)

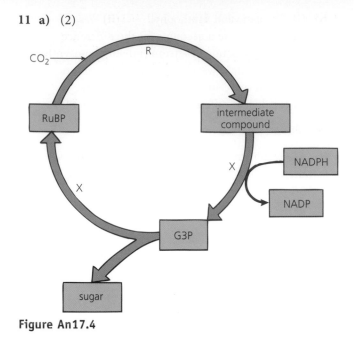

Figure An17.4

b) (i) RuBP **(ii)** and **(iii)** See figure in part **a)** (3)

c) (i) See figure in part **a)** **(ii)** To provide energy to drive the cycle (2)

d) (i) RuBP **(ii)** Because there would be no CO_2 present to which it could be combined to form the intermediate compound. (2)

e) (i) Intermediate compound **(ii)** Because there would be no ATP or NADPH to convert it to G3P. (2)

12 a) Light intensity (1)

b) Carbon dioxide concentration (1)

c) 20 times (1)

d) Temperature (1)

13 a) (i) 30 000 plants ha^{-1} **(ii)** 20 000 plants ha^{-1} (2)

b) (i) 2M : 2L **(ii)** 1M : 1L (2)

c) A crop of maize only and a crop of legumes only (1)

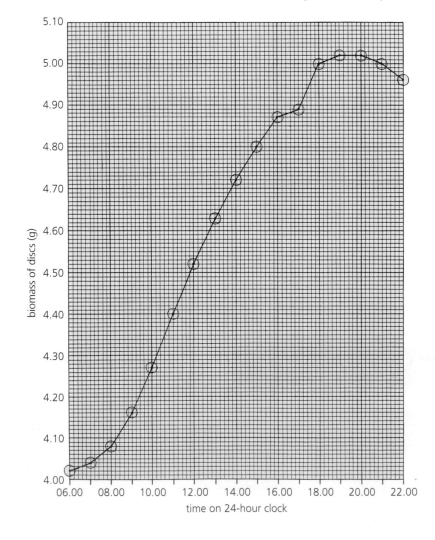

Figure An17.5

d) Repeat the experiment (1)

14 a) See Figure An17.5 (3)

b) 10.00–11.00 (1)

c) (i) 0.12 g (ii) 0.08 g (2)

d) Maybe it was sunnier in the morning or perhaps the stomata closed in the afternoon to conserve water but, by doing so, reduced the quantity of CO_2 able to enter for use in photosynthesis. (1)

e) Light intensity decreased as night approached thereby limiting the rate of photosynthesis. (1)

f) The same size of cork borer should be used every time to cut out the leaf discs. (1)

g) (i) 17.00 (ii) Perhaps human error was involved and some mistake was made. (2)

15 a) 36% (1)

b) Because the economic yield (the desired part of the harvest plant) is always less than the biological yield (the whole plant). (1)

16 See core text pages 236–238. (9)

18 Plant and animal breeding

1 a) Inflated is dominant because it has masked the appearance of constricted in the F_1 generation. (2)

b) Ii (1)

c) (4)

		Genotypes of pollen	
		I	i
Genotypes of ovules	I	II	Ii
	i	Ii	ii

Table An18.1

d) (i) 295 (ii) 590 (iii) 295 (3)

e) (i) Discrete (ii) It can be used to divide the population of pea plants into two distinct categories. (2)

2 a) A = RR, B = Rr, C = Rr, D = Rr, E = rr, F = rr (6)

b) Cross 3 (1)

3 a) 0 + 0 + 8 + 0 + 0 + 0 + 10 + 0 = 18 kg (1)

b) 6 + 6 + 0 + 0 + 3 + 0 + 10 + 10 = 35 kg (1)

c) $W^1w^1W^2w^2W^3w^3W^4w^4$ (1)

4 a) 2 (1)

b) (i) 3 (ii) 2 (2)

c) The plots were of equal size. (1)

d) Three replicates were set up. (1)

e) The treatments were randomised. (1)

f) (i) See Table An18.2 (ii) It is effective and helps the crop. This is demonstrated by the fact that the dry mass of plant material at harvest is greater for all plots with fungicide. (iii) As they stand, the results are not sufficiently different from one another to justify a conclusion being drawn in the absence of statistical analysis. (6)

g) The inclusion of plots without fertiliser (1)

5 No. Eventually all the alleles for the desirable features will have accumulated and the strain will not improve any further. (2)

6 a) 50% (1)

b) 25% (1)

c) A (1)

d) F_8 (1)

Fungicide or no fungicide	Fertiliser treatment (kg/acre)	Replicate 1	Replicate 2	Replicate 3
no fungicide	5	201	211	207
	35	304	312	305
	70	316	327	329
fungicide	5	252	258	249
	35	371	366	364
	70	379	383	386

Table An18.2

7 a) They were developed (by breeding and selection) as a crop suited to the warm conditions of Southern Europe. (2)

b) By a complicated breeding programme involving crosses between European and North American strains. (2)

c) It matures early therefore it is able to make the most of the short growing season. (1)

d) (i) Cattle and sheep **(ii)** Because it produces good solid cobs with high starch content that makes good animal feed. (3)

e) (i) Detach the male flower from A and shake the pollen onto the female flower of A, then isolate A in a greenhouse or inside a large transparent plastic bag. Repeat for B. **(ii)** Detach the male flower from A and shake the pollen onto the female flower of B. Detach the male flower from B and shake the pollen onto the female flower of A. Isolate A and B as before. (4)

8 The F_1 generation shows hybrid vigour. (2)

9 a) (2)

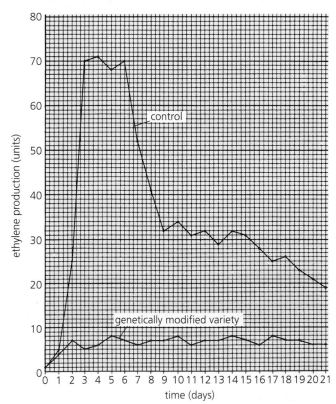

Figure An18.1

b) X = genetically modified, Y = control (1)

c) (i) 7 **(ii)** 70 (1)

d) 90% (1)

e) The tomato would fail to ripen. (1)

f) Genetically modified tomatoes have a longer shelf life. (1)

10 See core text pages 253–255 and 258–259. (9)

19 Crop protection

1 (7)

Weed species	Non-weed species
can grow well on poor soil	needs fertile soil to grow well
able to flower in any day length	requires short days to flower
quick to flower and produce many tiny seeds	slow to flower and produces a few large seeds
self-pollinated	cross-pollinated
tolerant of drought	intolerant of drought
tolerant of water-logged soil	intolerant of water-logged soil
short life cycle	long life cycle

Table An19.1

2 a) (i) = Q **(ii)** = S **(iii)** = P **(iv)** = R (3)

b) The wet areas could be drained and sprinklers could be used in the dry areas. (2)

c) Farmers could spray the chemical into the ground well in advance of planting the potatoes. The cysts would hatch and the larvae would emerge but die of starvation. (2)

d) (i) 7 years **(ii)** It would be more difficult for PCN to survive for 7 years than for 4 years waiting for the return of its host, the potato plant. (2)

3 a) (i) = 6 **(ii)** = 2 **(iii)** = 4 **(iv)** = 1 **(v)** = 5 (or 4) (5)

b) (i) Stage 6 **(ii)** The fungicide would kill the spores during the storage of the grain. (2)

4 a) (i) The yield increased with increased level of nitrogen. **(ii)** Nitrogen has been acting as a limiting factor. (2)

b) **(i)** The later the weeding, the poorer the grain yield.   **(ii)** Early season   **(iii)** If the weeds are removed early, the cereal has time to establish itself in the ground and then compete successfully with any weeds that return, therefore yield is affected less. (4)

c) 31.99 (1)

d) Other soil nutrients and water (2)

e) $340\,\mathrm{g\,m^{-2}}$ (1)

5 a) **(i)** and   **(ii)** B – I
D – A
G – E
H – C
J – F (4)

b) **(i)** and   **(ii)** Open-ended answer depending on the reader's opinion.

6 a) 12 (1)

b) 550 (1)

c) 19 times (1)

d) 166.67 (1)

e) **(i)** R   **(ii)** Fewer plants were infected. (2)

7 a) *Erysiphe graminis* and *Puccinia graminis* (1)

b) To improve the reliability of the results (1)

c) No significant effect by either A or B compared with the control (1)

d) Fungicide A had no effect at 5 ppm but worked to some extent at 50 ppm. Fungicide B had no effect at either concentration. (1)

e) **(i)** A   **(ii)** A   **(iii)** 50 ppm of A (2)

f) **(i)** 99   **(ii)** 38 (2)

g) They are effective on fungi W and X (that cause mildews) but have almost no effect on the other two fungi. (1)

h) A is more effective than B at killing spores of fungi W and X and it is less toxic to wildlife. (2)

8 a) They were resistant. (1)

b) Continued use of the *pesticide* over five years exerted a *selection pressure* and only those individuals that were members of the *resistant strain* survived by *natural selection*. In the absence of *competition* the resistant insects increased in number. (5)

9 a) wheat grain → seed-eating bird → peregrine falcon (1)

b) Dieldrin is non-biodegradable and therefore it builds up in concentration along the food chain as each organism eats a large number of the previous organism in the chain. (2)

c) C (1)

d) 65% (1)

e) Many thin-shelled eggs break during incubation so fewer young survive to become breeding adults. (1)

f) The number of breeding pairs is rising because use of dieldrin has been stopped and its effects are gradually disappearing. (1)

10 a) See core text pages 269–270. (3)

b) See core text pages 273–276. (4)

c) See core text pages 278–279. (2)

20 Animal welfare

1 a) **(i)** 1, 4, 5 and 7   **(ii)** 2, 3, 6 and 8 (2)

b) **(i)** Freedoms 3 and 4   **(ii)** They are not able to express their normal behaviour. They may injure themselves. (2)

c) Allow the cows out to graze in pastures for short periods over a few weeks in warm weather. (1)

2 a) **(i)** They are forms of behaviour that cannot be performed easily in an overcrowded cage but can be performed freely out of doors.   **(ii)** 4 and 7 (2)

b) 10 (risk of external parasites) (1)

c) **(i)** Uncaged   **(ii)** It includes an outside area where birds may peck at materials infected with parasites from wild birds. (2)

d) **(i)** Uncaged   **(ii)** They can move about freely therefore their bones develop strength. (2)

e) **(i)** The risk of it happening increases.
(ii) The caged birds express their stress by pecking one another's feathers and are able to do so freely if their beaks are left untrimmed. (2)

f) **(i)** Conventional = 11, furnished = 11, uncaged = 8
(ii) Install well-designed perches.
(iii) It would make the furnished and uncaged hen houses carry less risk, leaving the conventional cages carrying the most overall risk and the uncaged carrying the least overall risk. (4)

3 a) 3 (freedom from pain, injury and disease) (1)

b) **(i)** To kill bacteria that might cause disease   **(ii)** These would survive and might cause the disease which would then not be treatable by the antibiotic. (3)

c) **(i)** They must wear masks and protective clothing.   **(ii)** In the absence of a protective layer, the chemical could enter their bodies and cause serious harm. (2)

d) **(i)** $0.25\,g\,l^{-1}$ **(ii)** $25 \times 10^4\,\mu g\,l^{-1}$ (2)

e) **(i)** Draining the pasture and spraying it with molluscicide is preventative. Using drugs to kill the parasite inside the sheep is curative.   **(ii)** Prevention is better because it 'nips the problem in the bud', avoids stress and misery to the animal and is usually cheaper than tackling a disease epidemic. (3)

4 a) Ethogram (1)

b) 3 min 20 s (1)

c) (4)

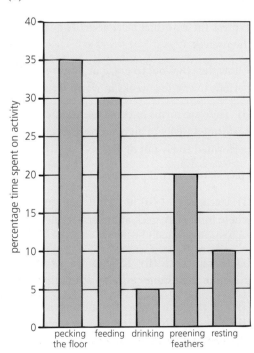

Figure An20.1

d) **(i)** 1, 2, 9, 10, 11, 17 and 18   **(ii)** Motivation (2)

e) **(i)** Repeat the series of observations with no food on the floor or with food in a shallow dish only.   **(ii)** If the chicken stopped pecking the floor or only pecked at the food in the dish, this would support the hypothesis. (2)

f) It would need to be repeated to see if the same results were obtained. (1)

5 a) Because they are housed in an environment that is overcrowded and lacking in basic facilities. (1)

b) (5)

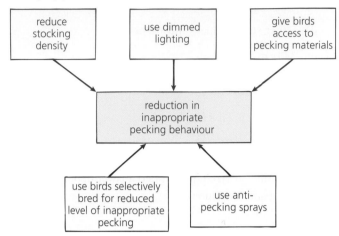

Figure An20.2

c) **(i)** Anti-pecking spray   **(ii)** Chain reaction of injurious pecking and cannibalism (2)

6 See core text pages 284–286. (9)

21 Symbiosis

1 Mutualism = **a)**, **d)**, **f)**   and **g)**; parasitism = **b)**, **c)**, **e)** and **h)** (4)

2 a) **(i)** It brings about an increase in growth rate.   **(ii)** Two weeks after the start of the experimental diet   **(iii)** It brought about a decrease in the growth rate.   **(iv)** Because the parasite is using some of the protein for its own growth. (4)

b) The adults took from week 2 to week 6 to breed and produce larvae. (1)

c) 6 times (1)

d) 166.67% (1)

e) Week 19 (1)

3 a) 27 °C (1)

b) **(i)** 1 and 2 = 100% healthy   **(ii)** 1 = 50% healthy, 25% bleached, 25% dead; 2 = 75% bleached, 25% dead (2)

c) **(i)** $0.85 \times 10^6\,cm^{-2}$ **(ii)** 0 (2)

d) **(i)** 1.4–$1.9 \times 10^6\,cm^{-2}$ **(ii)** No   **(iii)** Their ranges overlap. (3)

e) (i) $1.3–1.8 \times 10^6\,cm^{-2}$ (ii) Yes
(iii) Their ranges do not overlap. (3)

f) Initially there is no change then there is a sudden decrease at 32°C. (1)

g) There is a continuous decrease with increasing temperature. (1)

h) It is able to acquire some tolerance if it contains type A zooxanthellae but not if it contains type B. (1)

4 See core text pages 294–295. (9)

22 Social behaviour

1 a) 56 (1)

b) 15 (1)

c) 15 (1)

d) 6 (1)

e) The recipient's gain (1)

f) Reciprocal altruism (1)

2 a) (i) 2, 9 and 14   (ii) 3, 8, 10, 16 and 17
(iii) 4, 5, 11, 12 and 18   (iv) 1, 6, 7, 13, 15, 19 and 20 (4)

b) (i) 4, 5, 9, 11, 12 and 18   (ii) 3, 5, 10 and 12 (2)

c) 60 (1)

d) (i)

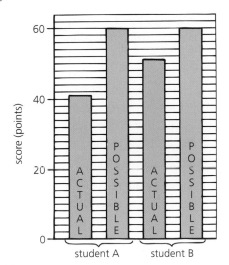

Figure An22.1

(ii) B beat A at the game. Both students would have achieved a higher score if they had cooperated throughout. (5)

e) Even knowing that *cooperation* results in the best outcome for the group as a whole, many players of the prisoner's *dilemma* find it difficult to reciprocate acts of *altruism* by choosing to *reduce* the sentence of their accomplice at the cost of staying a little *longer* in jail themselves. In the hope of achieving their personal optimal outcome, they tend to make *self-interested* decisions and continue to *betray* their accomplice which results in both players ending up *worse* off than they would have been by acting cooperatively. (4)

3 a) 2   b) 8   c) 4 (3)

4 a) Differences: In bees, the queen is fertilised by a drone to produce the next generation whereas in termites, a royal couple produce the next generation. In bees, the lower castes are composed of female workers and male drones whereas in termites, they are composed of workers and soldiers which both contain male and female members. Similarities: Only a minority of individuals contribute to the production of the next generation. Most members of the society are sterile but cooperate to raise the young of their close relatives. (4)

b) (i) Termites have cellulose-digesting bacteria in their gut that help them to make use of cellulose as a food. In return, the bacteria gain a food supply and a secure habitat.   (ii) Mutualism (3)

5 a) C, E, A, D, B (1)

b) Day 4 = C and E; day 17 = A and D (2)

c) 24 hours (1)

d) 20% (1)

e) (i) Day 23 = much foraging (70% of time) and little resting (20% of time); day 24 = little foraging (20% of time) and much resting (70% of time)
(ii) If it does a lot of foraging in a day then it only has time for a short rest that day therefore the next day it needs a longer rest and only has time for a little foraging. (4)

6 a) (i) The first female to become part of the group has the highest rank and so on to the last female to join the group, who has the lowest status.
(ii) The female with the lowest status (and any offspring that she has)   (iii) He would be unable to protect three females and their offspring all at once, so it is better if he concentrates on guarding one female and her young. (3)

b) (i) Young gorillas, on reaching puberty, emigrate from their troop of birth therefore they do not breed with their close relatives. (ii) When a son inherits a father's group (2)

7 a) (i) As age increases so does the ability to read emotions. (ii) Both genders of adult ape, but not the juveniles, chose the banana box more often than would be expected by chance alone. (iii) As apes grow older, they become more experienced at interpreting emotional expressions of the face. (3)

b) (i) There is no difference. (ii) The results for males and females do not appear to be significantly different for either age group (though further statistical analysis would be needed to verify this). (2)

c) So that an ape has to depend on his/her ability to read emotions to choose the banana box and does not learn by association which box contains the banana. (2)

8 See core text pages 307–308. (9)

23 Mass extinction and biodiversity

1 a) (i) C (ii) D (iii) B (iv) E (v) A (1)

b) D (1)

c) C (1)

d) B (1)

2 a) Proterozoic (1)

b) (i) Algae (ii) No (2)

c) (i) Devonian (ii) One which possesses transport tissue made of vessels (e.g. xylem). (2)

d) (i) Seed ferns and primitive conifers (ii) Seed ferns (3)

e) (i) Tree species (ii) The clearing of tropical rainforest is having a serious effect. (2)

3 a) (i) Trilobites (ii) Fish (2)

b) (i) Corals (ii) Fish (iii) Trilobites (3)

c) (i) 230 million years ago (ii) 220 million years ago (2)

d) (i) 65 million years ago (ii) Number of species of mammals increased. (iii) The evolution of milk to feed their young and an improved level of

parental care have increased their chance of survival and contributed to the rise in their numbers. (3)

4 It is possible that as the Earth became colder, all eggs were incubated at a lower temperature which produced one but not both sexes. This made reproduction impossible. (2)

5 a) (i) Yes (ii) Non-polluted has a higher number of different species. (2)

b) Non-polluted = 4.88; polluted = 1.99 (2)

6 a) Richness (1)

b) (i) 4 (ii) 2 (iii) 4 is nearest to the mainland whereas 2 is furthest away from the mainland. (3)

c) No change (1)

d) (i) 4 (ii) 5 (2)

e) (i) H (ii) E (2)

24 Threats to biodiversity

1 a) 4 years (1)

b) (i) Decrease in the total number of plaice caught (ii) The stocks are being overfished. (2)

c) The '11 years' entry refers to one year only; the '12+ years' entry refers to the sum of several years. (1)

d) A greater number of younger fish were caught in years 4 and 5. (2)

e) If the catch continues to get younger, eventually there will be no adult fish left to produce future stocks. (2)

f) 70% (1)

2 a) (i) It has rapidly expanded its geographical range and the variety of flower species upon which it feeds. (ii) It is closely adapted to a particular habitat and is unable to change. (iii) Chequered skipper (4)

b) The area is so fragmented by human activity that the butterfly is unable to cover the distance between one unspoiled habitat fragment and another. (2)

c) (i) As the climate becomes warmer, the butterfly seeks cooler habitats up the hills. (ii) If global warming continues, it will eventually run out of high-altitude habitats and face extinction. (2)

d) Agriculture/urbanisation (1)

3 a) 7.33 (1)

b) 140 000 (1)

c) 8400 (1)

d) 16.00 (1)

e) 1 500 000 (1)

4 a) **(i)** Invasive   **(ii)** It has brought about the extinction of native freshwater mussels. (2)

b) **(i)** It cuts fishing lines/injures swimmers. **(ii)** It blocks water intakes to hydroelectric schemes. (2)

c) **(i)** Algae   **(ii)** They grow better because more light for photosynthesis reaches them through the clearer water. (2)

d) **(i)** Roach   **(ii)** Crayfish (2)

e) Stock the lake with fish such as smallmouth bass and yellow perch which would eat the zebra mussels. (1)

f) Continuous (1)

5 a) See core text pages 325–326. (3)

b) See core text pages 326–327 (3)

c) See core text pages 328–329. (3)